AF731395

ZEW Economic Studies

Publication Series of the Centre for European Economic Research (ZEW), Mannheim, Germany

ZEW Economic Studies

Vol. 1: O. Hohmeyer, K. Rennings (Eds.)
Man-Made Climate Change
Economic Aspects and Policy Options
1999. VIII, 401 pp. ISBN 3-7908-1146-7

Vol. 2: Th. Büttner
Agglomeration, Growth, and Adjustment
A Theoretical and Empirical Study
of Regional Labor Markets in Germany
1999. XI, 206 pp. ISBN 3-7908-1160-2

Vol. 3: P. Capros et al.
Climate Technology Strategies 1
Controlling Greenhouse Gases.
Policy and Technology Options
1999. XVIII, 365 pp. ISBN 3-7908-1229-3

Vol. 4: P. Capros et al.
Climate Technology Strategies 2
The Macro-Economic Cost and Benefit
of Reducing Greenhouse Gas Emissions
in the European Union
1999. XIII, 224 pp. ISBN 3-7908-1230-7

Vol. 5: P.A. Puhani
Evaluating Active Labour Market Policies
Empirical Evidence for Poland During
Transition
1999. XVI, 239 pp. ISBN 3-7908-1234-X

Vol. 6: B. Fitzenberger
Wages and Employment Across Skill Groups
An Analysis for West Germany
1999. XII, 251 pp. ISBN 3-7908-1235-8

Vol. 7: K. Rennings et al. (Eds.)
Social Costs and Sustainable Mobility
Strategies and Experiences in Europe
and the United States
1999. VI, 212 pp. ISBN 3-7908-1260-9

Vol. 8: H. Legler et al.
Germany's Technological Performance
2000. X, 191 pp. ISBN 3-7908-1281-1

Vol. 9: O. Bürgel
The Internationalization of British Start-up Companies in High-Technology Industries
2000. XIV, 230 pp. ISBN 3-7908-1292-7

Vol. 10: J. Hemmelskamp et al. (Eds.)
Innovation-Oriented Environmental Regulation
Theoretical Approaches and Empirical
Analysis
2000. VI, 348 pp. ISBN 3-7908-1313-3

Vol. 11: K.L. Brockmann, M. Stronzik (Eds.)
Flexible Mechanisms
for an Efficient Climate Policy
Cost Saving Policies and Business
Opportunities
2000. VIII, 130 pp. ISBN 3-7908-1314-1

Vol. 12: W. Smolny
Endogenous Innovations
and Knowledge Spillovers
A Theoretical and Empirical Analysis
2000. VIII, 277 pp. ISBN 3-7908-1320-6

Vol. 13: M. Lechner, F. Pfeiffer (Eds.)
Econometric Evaluation
of Labour Market Policies
2001. X, 242 pp. ISBN 3-7908-1372-9

Vol. 14: M. Beise
Lead Markets
Country-Specific Success Factors of the
Global Diffusion of Innovations
2001. XVI, 305 pp. ISBN 3-7908-1430-X

Otto H. Jacobs · Christoph Spengel

Effective Tax Burden in Europe

Current Situation, Past Developments and Simulations of Reforms

With 10 Figures
and 39 Tables

Physica-Verlag
A Springer-Verlag Company

ZEW
Zentrum für Europäische
Wirtschaftsforschung GmbH
Centre for European
Economic Research

Series Editor
Prof. Dr. Wolfgang Franz

Authors

Prof. Dr. Dr. h.c. mult. Otto H. Jacobs
Dr. Christoph Spengel
Universität Mannheim
Lehrstuhl für Allgemeine Betriebswirtschaftslehre,
Treuhandwesen und Betriebswirtschaftliche Steuerlehre II
Schloß
68131 Mannheim
Germany

ISBN 978-3-7908-1470-5 ISBN 978-3-642-51036-6 (eBook)
DOI 10.1007/978-3-642-51036-6

Cataloging-in-Publication Data applied for
Die Deutsche Bibliothek – CIP-Einheitsaufnahme
Jacobs, Otto H.; Spengel, Christoph: Effective Tax Burden in Europe. – Heidelberg; New York: Physica-Verl., 2002
(ZEW economic studies; Vol. 15)
ISBN 978-3-7908-1470-5

Physica-Verlag Heidelberg New York
a member of BertelsmannSpringer Science+Business Media GmbH

Cover design: Erich Dichiser, ZEW, Mannheim

SPIN 10864163 88/2202-5 4 3 2 1 0 – Printed on acid-free paper

Preface

Our small book presents a report which has been prepared in the year 2000 for the Taxation and Customs Union Directorate General of the European Commission, under contract no. TAXUD / 00 / 312. Some of the results form part of the report "Company Taxation in the Internal Market" of the Commission Services released in autumn 2001.

We present estimates of effective average tax rates (EATR) in five EU Member States (France, Germany, Ireland, the Netherlands and the UK) plus the USA based on the European Tax Analyzer approach. The European Tax Analyzer is a computer based model firm approach for the computation and comparison of international company tax burdens. It has been developed in co-operation with the Centre for European Economic Research (ZEW).

We would like to thank the ZEW for this co-operation. Furthermore, we gratefully acknowledge the help and advice of *Gerd Gutekunst*, *Rico A. Hermann* and *Thorsten Stetter* in preparing the report. Special mention must be made of *Gerd Gutekunst*, who was also responsible for preparing the printed version of this report.

Mannheim, October 2001 *Otto H. Jacobs* and *Christoph Spengel*

Contents

Executive Summary

Introduction

During the past years, various measures to compute and to compare effective tax burdens of companies have been developed. The accuracy of the results of tax burden comparisons depends on the methodological approach which is used for the computation. The most meaningful indicators for the effective levels of taxation are derived from forward-looking concepts. With respect to the type of investment we can distinguish between the effective marginal and the effective average tax rate. The standard model for the calculation of the effective *marginal* tax rate (EMTR) is the well known approach of King and Fullerton. This approach has been applied in the most important international studies on the effective tax burden of companies in the past decade, for example, in the Ruding Report. By contrast, no standard model exists for the calculation of the effective average tax rate (EATR). However, the EATR is of high empirical relevance for location and financing decisions of companies.

Purpose and structure of the report

This report presents estimates of effective average tax rates (EATR) in five EU Member States (France, Germany, Ireland, the Netherlands, and the UK) plus – for the sake of comparison – the USA based on the European Tax Analyzer approach. The *European Tax Analyzer* is a computer based model firm approach for the computation and comparison of international company tax burdens. Since the model firm is designed as a corporation, the tax burden can be calculated at the level of the corporation as well as at the level of the shareholders. The EATR is derived by simulating the development of a corporation over a ten year period. For the computation of the tax burden the model takes into account the most relevant and complex provisions of the tax regimes. The comparison in this report is restricted to domestic investment and thus excludes cross-border investment.

The main aim of the study is to compute and compare EATR on investment by a domestic company in different locations. A secondary aim is to work out the impact of the different tax drivers on the effective tax burden, i.e. to show how the EATR is influenced by the tax systems, the different types of (profit and non-profit) taxes, the tax bases and the tax rates. The comparison of the EATR is made in two stages. Section 2 determines and compares the EATR in the different countries taking as a base case a typical medium-sized manufacturing company. Section 3 examines how the results will be affected by alternative assumptions on the economic data of the company.

Up to this stage the study uses information about the tax systems in operation as of the fiscal year 1999. Section 4 analyses the effects of the German tax reform that became effective from 1 January 2001. Based on this information, section 5 recalculates the EATR beginning with the fiscal year 1995 in order to highlight the most important tax reforms in the past. Section 6 analyses the effects of hypothetical tax reforms. In order to gain an impression regarding how the EATRs in different countries are influenced by the underlying methodological approach, section 7 compares the results obtained by the European Tax Analyzer with those that would be obtained by the approach of Devereux and Griffith. This model was used in another report for European Commission on the effective levels of company taxation in the European Union.

Results for the base case scenario

Section 2 compares the EATR for a typical base case. This base case considers a medium-sized corporation with economic data that is typical for the manufacturing sector. With respect to the tax burden at the *level of the corporation* the results reveal a considerable range of the EATR from 39.7% in France to 8.3% in Ireland. Germany (32.8%), the Netherlands (24%) and the UK (21%) range in between. The average EATR of the EU Member States is 25.2%; the EATR of the US corporation amounts to 29.7%.

The corporation tax has by far the highest impact on the EATR. Although there is a large variation between the domestic corporation tax bases, the ranking of the countries with respect to the effective tax burden closely follows the level of the statutory tax rates on profits. Since there exist no considerable non-profit taxes, in general, the profit taxes have by far the highest impact on the effective tax burden. The only exception is France with a high portion of non-profit taxes. This is also the reason why the structure of the French tax system differs significantly from the other countries.

If *personal taxes* are *included*, the range of the EATR becomes even higher. This suggests that there is more variation in personal taxes than in corporate taxes. Besides the level of corporate taxes, the differences in the presence of personal taxes can be attributed to the corporation tax systems, the average income tax rates and the levy of capital taxes. However, the country ranking with reference to the EATR is the same as at the level of corporation.

Sensitivity analysis

Since the effective tax burden always depends on individual cases it is impossible to make universally valid statements regarding the differences between the EATR across countries. Therefore, section 3 carries out a number of sensitivity analyses. At the level of the corporation we considered alternative assumptions on the investment policy, the structure of finance and the profitability of the company as well as on the industry as a whole. In so doing, the EATRs of 10 other industries were calculated. At the shareholder level, we considered alternative assumptions regarding the distribution policy of the company and the sources of company finance provided by the shareholders.

The broad conclusions that were drawn for the base case with reference to the *corporation level* do not seem to be affected. It has to be stressed, however, that the relative position of the countries cannot be generalised. At the *shareholder level*, in contrast to the corporation level, there is much more variation in the EATR and the country ranking. Therefore, it is not possible to make universally valid statements about the EATR at the overall level. One can, however, draw a broad conclusion concerning the average EATR of the EU Member States. The average EATR converges (diverges) as more profits are distributed to the shareholders (retained in the corporation). Thus, differences between corporate and personal taxes and the corporation tax systems seem to be minimised in situations where most of the corporate profits are also subject to personal taxes. Another result of the sensitivity analyses (which is confirmed by many other studies) is that the tax systems of the countries covered by this report are far from neutral. The results clearly show that taxation distorts corporations' investment and financing decisions in every country. It is important to note that, in general, the lower the statutory tax rates, the lower these distortions tend to be.

Effects of the German tax reform 2001

The German tax reform became effective in January 2001. It is an important tax reform within the EU since it replaces the full imputation tax system and introduces a shareholder relief system, reduces the corporate and personal income tax rates and finally broadens the tax base. Therefore, the effects of the German tax reform are analysed in section 4.

However, the considerable reduction of the EATR at the *level of the corporation* has only minor effects. Although the EATR falls by 8.2%, Germany cannot improve its position in the country ranking. The sensitivity analyses including 10 other selected industries shows that companies with capital intensive production and high distribution ratios will even suffer from the results of the German tax reform. By contrast, companies with personnel intensive production and a high ratio of retained profits will benefit. However, even with respect to the additional 10 companies, the changes in Germany's country ranking are only minor.

With reference to the taxation of the *shareholders*, there is a significant reduction in the EATR only if one takes a medium-sized company as typical. By contrast, the EATR is likely to rise for a (multinational) company with a high number of domestic shareholders.

Changes of the effective average tax burden since 1995

Section 5 summarises the main tax reforms and their consequences for the EATR since 1995. There is some evidence that in particular those countries which had or still have a relatively high EATR are demonstrating a tendency towards a significant reduction in their effective tax burdens (e.g. Germany and France). The dominant trend in the decrease of the EATR has been a reduction in the statutory tax rates on profits. However, tax rate reductions were not the only reason for the decrease of the EATR. From a systematic point of view, the gradual abolition of non-profit taxes and the trend towards an implementation of shareholder relief corporation tax systems have to be emphasised.

As a result of the reforms the average EATR have converged both at the corporation level and the overall level. Since countries with relatively low EATRs did not reduce their tax burden remarkably, however, there is no so-called race to the bottom. In spite of the gradual convergence of the EATR one cannot conclude, that tax distortions due to competition disappeared. Instead, the differences between the EATR are still high.

Impact of hypothetical tax reforms in the EU

A major finding of the analysis of the existing tax regimes is that they are designed as more or less integrated systems. This means that there is a particular relationship between the tax rate, the tax base and the corporation tax system. It is therefore clear that a neutral tax regime across EU Member States can only be reached by simultaneously strictly harmonising the tax rates, tax bases, taxes and corporation tax systems. However, this option – which is, in fact, a full harmonisation – is not at all feasible or realistic. By contrast, more practical solutions concentrate on co-ordinating only certain elements of the tax regimes. In doing so, it is above all necessary to understand the weights of each of the most important elements of a tax regime in the effective tax burden. Therefore, section 6 has been aimed at analysing the impact of the corporation tax base, the corporation tax rate including surcharges and local taxes, and the corporation tax system on the EATR in separate steps. The main findings of the simulations are as follows:

A. Introducing a *common corporate tax base* clearly helps to achieve more transparency in the calculation of effective tax burdens. However, such a change would result in increasing the dispersion of the EATR across EU Member States since the impact of the other elements of the tax regimes on the EATR increases (e.g. the tax rates).

B. Similarly, a *common corporation tax system* also tends to increase the dispersion of the EATR across EU Member States.

C. By contrast, the introduction of a *common statutory tax rate on profits* would significantly reduce the dispersion of the EATR across the EU Member States. None of the other hypothetical reforms considered here reduced the variation of the effective tax burdens in a comparable way.

Comparison of the European Tax Analyzer results with the results obtained by the model of Devereux and Griffith

Different models exist for the calculation of the EATR. Section 7 has compared the results derived by the European Tax Analyzer with the results derived by the Devereux-Griffith model. The latter approach was applied in a parallel report for the European Commission on the same subject. The two approaches differ with respect to their economic models, the tax variables included in the models and the techniques for calculating the EATR. Therefore, it is almost impossible to arrive at the same EATR even in the event of an identical tax regime.

Nonetheless, the comparison of the most important results computed for domestic investment revealed that neither the main conclusions in this report nor in the other report based on the Devereux-Griffith model are affected by the methodology to a great extent. This was shown for the base case scenario, the effects of the German tax reform 2001 and the implications of a number of hypothetical tax reforms.

Final conclusion

The comparison of the EATRs for a typical medium-sized corporation as well as various sensitivity analyses for alternative assumptions of both economic and tax data reveal a wide spread between the effective tax burden in different EU Member States. The levels of the EATRs and the differences between EU Member States depend on individual circumstances of a company such as, for example, profitability, types of investment and sources of finance. It has been shown that the tax regimes can distort competition with respect to location, financing and investment decisions to a considerable extent. These distortions are the result of the different types of taxes, tax rates, tax bases and corporation tax systems. It could be worked out that from these elements of a tax regime the statutory tax rate on profits in general has the highest impact on the level of the EATR and the differences between the EATRs across EU Member States.

1 Introduction

1.1 Background, aim and structure of the study

The European Commission has received a mandate from the Council for a study on company taxation in the EU. This study is to illuminate, among other things, existing differences in effective levels of corporate taxation in the EU.

In order to measure the effective tax burden, various methodological approaches have been developed and applied in the past. It has been shown elsewhere (e.g. OECD, 2000a) that the best indicators for the effective levels of taxation are derived from forward-looking concepts. In contrast to backward-looking concepts which refer to data accumulated in the past,[1] forward-looking approaches refer to hypothetical future projects. Depending on the type of investment and its return respectively, we can distinguish between the effective *marginal* tax rate (EMTR) and the effective average tax rate (EATR). Whereas the EMTR measures the extra tax of an additional (marginal) project that is just worthwhile (i.e. the presumed rate of return equals the cost of capital) the EATR measures the effective tax burden of projects that earn more than the capital costs (i.e. projects generating economic rents or positive net present values of the firm/investment).

The standard model for the calculation of the EMTR is the well known approach of King and Fullerton (1984) that focuses on the taxation of single investments financed in specific ways. The underlying idea of this model was recently extended by Devereux and Griffith (1999) who have developed an approach for the calculation of the EATR. A completely different method for the calculation of the EATR is the model-firm approach which, in its simplest way, can be characterised as a firm-specific combination of several investments (assets) and sources of finance taking into account at the same time all relevant interrelations between sales (rate of return), investment, profit distribution and financing etc. In fact, the model-firm approach was already applied by the OECD (1985) many years ago, but only on a one period basis. It was mainly the joint research of the Centre for European Economic Research (ZEW) and the University of Mannheim that extended this approach to a multi-period computer model, the European Tax Analyzer (Spengel, 1995; Jacobs and Spengel, 1996; Meyer, 1996).

This report presents estimates of effective average tax rates (EATR) in five EU Member States (France, Germany, Ireland, the Netherlands, and the UK) plus – for the sake of comparison – the USA based on the European Tax Analyzer approach. The main aim of the study is to compute and compare EATR on

---

1 The data referred to could be the capital stock, profits or data derived from financial statements of companies.

investment by a domestic company in different locations.[2] A secondary aim is to work out the impact of the different tax drivers on the effective tax burden, i.e. to show how the EATR is influenced by the tax systems, the different types of (profit and non-profit) taxes, the tax bases and the tax rates.

The remainder of this introduction summarises the methodological approach taken in the study. The comparison of the EATR is made in two stages. Section 2 determines and compares the EATR in the different countries taking as a base case a typical medium-sized manufacturing company. The main focus is on company taxes. The personal taxes of the (private) domestic shareholders will be taken into account separately. This distinction is mainly justified by the fact that the role of personal taxes for investment decisions is not always clear. Moreover, it is possible to identify the impact of corporate and personal taxes on the overall tax burden separately and see the interaction of corporate and personal taxes. Section 3 examines how the results will be affected by alternative assumptions on the economic data of the company. Up to this stage the study uses information about the tax systems in operation as of the fiscal year 1999. Section 4 analyses the effects of the German tax reform that became effective from 1 January 2001 and compares the results with those of the base case scenario. Based on this information, section 5 recalculates the EATR beginning with the fiscal year 1995 up to the year 2001 both at the level of the company and the shareholders (overall level). This summarises the consequences of the main tax reforms during this period. Section 6 analyses the effects of hypothetical tax reforms. We consider three elements of the national tax regimes: the corporation tax base, the corporation tax rate including local taxes and the corporation tax system. In order to gain an impression regarding how the EATR in different countries are influenced by the underlying methodological approach, section 7 compares the results obtained by the European Tax Analyzer with those that would be obtained by the approach of Devereux and Griffith. This model was used in another report for European Commission on the effective levels of company taxation in the European Union (see Devereux, Lammersen and Spengel, 2000). Section 8 includes a summary of the main conclusions.

1.2 Methodological concept of the European Tax Analyzer

The European Tax Analyzer is a computer program for a model-firm. It calculates and compares effective average tax burdens for companies located in different countries. Since the model firm is designed as a corporation, the tax burden can be calculated at the level of the corporation as well as at the level of the shareholders. The effective average tax burden is derived by simulating the development of a corporation over a ten year period. For the computation of the tax burden the

---

2 Cross-border investments are not taken into account.

model uses the economic data of the corporation and the shareholders as well as tax data as inputs.

The development of the corporation is based on the initial capital stock and the data of the corporate plans containing variable estimates for the future development of the capital stock.

A. *Initial capital stock*: The capital stock in the first period includes the firm's total assets and liabilities that either can be new or already existing. The *assets* consist of real estate, office and production buildings, plant and machinery, office furnishings, fixtures, intangibles (patents and royalties), financial assets, shares in other corporations (both domestic and foreign), inventories, trade debtors, cash funds, and deposits. The *liabilities* include new equity capital, long-term and short-term debt, and trade creditors.

B. *Development of capital stock*: *Corporate planning* supplies data about the expected development of the capital stock over the simulation period of ten years. The estimates are based on periodical assumptions for production and sales, acquisition of goods, staff expenditure (e.g. number of employees, wage per employee and pension costs), other receipts and expenses (e.g. R&D-expenses), investment, distribution, and costs of financing. It is assumed that in each period the corporation produces goods which are either inventoried or sold on the market. Therefore, multi-period production is possible. Additional variable assumptions are made with regard to the production costs for material and labour. It is further assumed that depreciable assets (i.e. buildings, plant and machinery, office furnishing, fixtures, and intangibles) are worn out at the end of their expected economic life. Optionally, fixed assets can also be sold for their market value before the end of expected economic life. In either of the two cases, reinvestments in new assets are made at that time based on the historical costs of the assets adjusted for inflation. The model's assumptions regarding investment ensure that the initial capital stock at least remains constant.[3] In addition to differing rates of price increases, other macro-economic data considered are credit and debit interest rates, exchange rates for the given countries and the costs of energy and electricity.

C. *Corporate finance*: The initial capital stock contains new equity as well as both long and short term debt capital. Since the corporate plans, inter alia, make assumptions about the distribution policy, the company can be financed by retained earnings (e.g. the distribution rate is below 100%) in addition to new equity and debt financing. Moreover, if the national tax codes allow for internal book reserves (e.g. book reserves for bad debts), the money put into these reserves also serves as a source of internal financing.

---

3 It is also possible to allow additional new investment which results in an increase of the capital stock during the simulation period.

Due to differences between the corporation tax systems as well as the taxation of capital income (e.g. dividends, interest, and capital gains) in the hands of the *shareholders,* a valid comparison of the tax burdens has to include the shareholders. The model allows the inclusion of up to 10 groups of shareholders with different shareholding (e.g. participation rate) and personal status. The latter distinguishes between natural and legal persons, domestic or foreign shareholders, taxable or tax-exempt entities, and other aspects (e.g. family status, number of children). According to the financing of the corporation, the shareholders receive dividends from new equity or interest from loans to the corporation. In addition to this income, the underlying assets (e.g. shares and loans) are considered for non-profit taxes.

For the sake of comparability, it is assumed that the model-firm in each country shows identical data before any taxation. Due to this necessary assumption any differences between pre- and post-tax data in the model can be solely attributed to taxation in the different countries.

The tax burden is expressed in two ways: The *absolute effective average tax burden* in currency units is the difference between the pre-tax and the post-tax value of the firm at the end of the simulation period (i.e. period 10). An equivalent expression of the effective average tax burden is the *effective average tax rate* (EATR). The EATR is the difference between the pre-tax and the post-tax return on the equity capital invested in the corporation divided by the pre-tax return. These returns are derived from the value of the firm at the end of the simulation period. The effective average tax burden is calculated separately for the level of the corporation and the level of the shareholders (if their taxation is included). The computation of total tax burdens and the EATR takes four steps.

In the *first step*, the pre-tax value of the firm at the end of the simulation period is calculated. The pre-tax value of the firm is derived from the estimated cash flows and the value of the net assets at the end of the simulation period. The cash flows are derived from estimates in the corporate planing for the cash receipts (sales and other receipts, gains upon the disposal of assets, interest and dividend income) and expenses (wages and pension payments, expenses for material, energy consumption and other expenses, new investment, interest expenses and distributed profits). The cash flow (= liquidity) is calculated in each period. Thereby it is assumed that any given amount of surplus cash flow at the end of a single period can be invested at a given interest rate and any given deficit can by covered by borrowing money at a given debit rate (balancing investment or credit). The interest receipts or expenses plus the amount of the underlying balancing investments or credits are considered for the calculation of the cash flow in the following period. The value of the net assets at the end of the simulation period is computed by deducting the liabilities of the corporation (and, if relevant, of the shareholders) from the assets. Both the assets and the liabilities are valued at calibrated parameters that are the same in each country. For the assets we take their replacement prices and for the liabilities their nominal values.

	pre-tax cash flow at the end of the simulation period (companies' or overall level)
+	value of the net assets at the end of the simulation period (companies' or overalllevel) (= assets in the capital stock at replacement prices - liabilities in the capital stock at nominal values)
=	pre-tax value of the firm at the end of the simulation period (companies' or overall level)

In the *second step,* the post-tax value of the firm at the end of the simulation period is calculated. The determination of the post-tax value of the firm has only cash flow effects and no impact on the value of the net assets. The post-tax cash flow is derived in each period by deducting the tax liabilities from the pre-tax cash flow. The tax liabilities are derived by transforming the receipts and expenses into items of the tax bases (i.e. on the one hand assets and liabilities and on the other hand profits and losses/charges) respect given to depreciation allowances according to the relevant national rules and then applying the (functions of the) tax rates and, if necessary, other relevant provisions (e.g. loss carryover and tax credits). The reduction of the cash flow due to tax payments (liabilities) also has an impact on the balancing investment or credit and the connected interest receipts or credits. By taking these tax-induced effects on the interest income or expense of each period into account, the deferral of tax payments is integrated into the model.

	pre-tax cash flow at the end of the simulation period (companies' or overall level)
-	tax liabilities in each period
=	post-tax cash flow at the end of the simulation period (companies' or overall level)
+	value of the net assets at the end of the simulation period (companies' or overall level) (= assets in the capital stock at replacement prices – liabilities in the capital stock at nominal values)
=	post-tax value of the firm at the end of the simulation period (companies' or overall level)
	Pre-tax value of the firm at the end of the simulation period

	(companies' or overall level)
-	post-tax value of the firm at the end of the simulation period (companies' or overall level)
=	total average tax burden in currency units (companies' or overall level)

In contrast to models which compute tax burdens solely based on pre-tax returns (yields), calculations based on cash receipts and cash expenses considering balancing investments allow the entire computation of all tax bases at any time during the period of simulation (because all relevant income and assets have been entered into the tax base). As a consequence, the model can include complicated tax provisions such as progressive tax rates, tax credits (e.g. for foreign taxes) with upper ceilings, and loss carryovers without any difficulty.

In the *third step,* both the pre-tax and the post-tax value of the firm at the end of the simulation period are transformed into the pre-tax and post-tax return respectively:

$$r = [V_f(T) / V_i(0)]^{1/T} - 1 \quad \text{and}$$

$$r_s = [V_{fs}(T) / V_i(0)]^{1/T} - 1$$

r = pre-tax return

r_s = post-tax return

V_i = value of the firm at beginning of the simulation period

V_f = pre-tax value of the firm at the end of the simulation period

V_{fs} = post-tax value of the firm at the end of the simulation period

T = simulation period

The return r (r_s) represents the internal rate of growth of the value of the firm during the simulation period before taxes (after taxes) taking into account all the assumptions about the investment, financing and distribution policy at the beginning of the simulation.

In the *fourth step*, the effective average tax rate (EATR) is computed by deducting the post-tax return from the pre-tax return and dividing this difference by the pre-tax return.

$$\frac{r - r_s}{r} = \text{EATR}$$

The EATR is measured as the difference between the pre-tax and the post-tax value of the firm or the return derived from the changes of the value of the firm. A cross-country comparison can thus allow for the following conclusion. A higher EATR indicates that taxation takes away a higher share of the pre-tax value of the firm (or the return). This may indicate as a result that countries with a higher EATR will be less attractive as a location for the firm than a country with a lower EATR.[4]

1.3 Tax parameters incorporated into the model

The EATR is calculated for companies in France, Germany, Ireland, the Netherlands, the UK and the USA. In order to calculate the tax liability in each country the European Tax Analyzer takes into account all *taxes* that may be influenced by the investments and financing both at the level of the corporation and the level of the shareholders (see Table 1). A detailed description of the tax parameters is not given here. Instead they are explained in the following sections when the EATR in the different countries are compared.

In calculating the *tax bases*, the most relevant elements with regard to the assets and liabilities included in the capital stock and the effects of the corporate planning are considered. Furthermore, the tax module of the model allows the selection of several accounting options (tax electives) enabling a company to influence its taxable profits. The *rules for profit computation* cover:

A. depreciation (methods and tax periods for all considered assets, extraordinary depreciation),
B. inventory (stock) valuation (production costs, FIFO, LIFO and the average costs method, inflation reserves),
C. development costs (immediate expensing or capitalisation),
D. taxation of capital gains (roll-over relief, inflation adjustment, special tax rates),
E. employee pension schemes (deductibility of pension costs, contributions to pension funds, book reserves),
F. provisions for bad debts,
G. elimination and mitigation of double taxation on foreign source income (exemption, foreign tax credit, deduction of foreign taxes),
H. and loss relief.

---

4 This interpretation is similar to the interpretation of the EATR in the model of Devereux and Griffith. See Bond and Chennells (2000: 15). It is of high empirical relevance since managers admit that they choose an investment location by comparing the post tax returns of similar location opportunities. See Luther (1994).

Table 1: Considered taxes

	Company	Shareholder
FRA	Taxe foncière *(real property tax)* Taxe professionnelle *(trade tax)* Taxes assises sur les salaires *(employer's contributions)* Impôt sur les sociétés *(corporation tax)*	Impôt sur le revenue *(income tax)* Prélèvements fiscaux *(surcharges on income tax)* Impôt de solidarité sur la fortune *(property tax)*
GER	Grundsteuer (real property tax) Gewerbeertragsteuer (trade tax on profits) Körperschaftsteuer (corporation tax) Solidaritätszuschlag (solidarity levy)	Einkommensteuer (income tax) Solidaritätszuchlag (solidarity levy) Kirchensteuer (church tax)
IRL	Business rates Corporation tax	Income tax
NL	Vennootschapsbelasting (corporation tax) Onroerendbelasting (real property tax)	Inkomstenbelasting (income tax) Vermogensbelasting (property tax)
UK	Business rates Corporation tax	Income tax
USA	Property tax Franchise tax on corporate income Accumulated earnings tax Corporate income tax	Income tax Property tax

Finally, referring to the *tax rates*, the calculations consider statutory linear as well as progressive tax rate structures. In the case of progressive rates or income brackets the tax rates enter in the model as functions of the relevant income or net assets (non-profit taxes) as provided by the tax laws. As far as Ireland is concerned, the base-case scenario takes into account the manufacturing relief resulting in a statutory corporation tax rate of 10%. The Appendix shows also the results for the basic 28% Irish corporation tax rate.

1.4 Structure of the model-firm and other economic assumptions for the base case

Various assumptions have to be made in order to define and describe the model-firm analysed in this report, and the economic conditions which are assumed to prevail. The following is assumed in the base case (section 2). Later, section 3 performs a sensitivity analysis in order to test the importance of these assumptions.

Table 2: Model firm's structure of the balance sheet (period 6)

Assets	Euro	**Liabilities**	Euro
A. Fixed assets		A. Shareholders' equity	
I. Intangible assets	647,898	*I. Share capital*	3,067,751
II. Tangible fixed assets		*II. Profit brought forward*	5,146,276
1. Real estate	4,017,936	*III. Net income*	1,367,177
2. Machinery	2,623,644	B. Provisions for Pensions	3,269,915
3. Office furniture and fixtures	1,337,024	C. Creditors	
		I. Loans from third parties	8,180,670
III. Financial assets		*II. Loans from shareholders*	1,533,876
1. Investments	5,112,919	*III. Trade creditors*	2,327,868
2. Long-term loans	766,938	*IV. Short-term debt*	10,021,321
B. Current assets			
I. Stock	7,523,749		
II. Trade debtors	7,049,872		
III. Fund's assets	3,269,915		
IV. Deposits	2,564,959		
Total	34,914,854	Total	34,914,854

Table 3: Model firm's structure of the profit and loss account (period 6)

	Position	Euro
	Net sales or revenues	44,061,700
–	Cost of goods sold	35,031,442
=	Gross profit	9,030,258
–	Selling expenses	1,389,415
–	General and administrative expenses	3,969,264
+	Other revenues	2,607,339
–	Other expenses	3,908,701
+	Investment earnings (dividends)	577,029
+	Interest income	225,620
–	Interest expenses	582,873
=	Operating income	2,589,993
–	Income tax expenses (if deductible)	401,154
–	Other taxes	2,718
=	Taxable income (income before corporation tax)	2,186,121

As a base case for the model-firm we refer to a typical medium-sized German[5] manufacturing company. The data was taken from published German statistics.[6] Table 2 shows the balance sheet and Table 3 the profit and loss account at the end of year six (the mid-point of the ten year comparison) based on the assumption of German taxation. Table 2 shows the different types of assets (investments) and sources of finance considered here in detail. It also serves to highlight the relative weight of these investments and sources of finance. Table 3 shows the sales and the amounts and structure of the expenses. From this information we can derive the following most important financial ratios of the base case model-firm:

---

5 The reason for taking Germany is simply the easy availability of reliable data. From a methodological point of view it would be no problem to use any other data instead.

6 See Deutsche Bundesbank (1997a), Deutsche Bundesbank (1997b), Industriekreditbank (1997), Statistisches Bundesamt (1997: 193-195, 206-207, 228-230, 464).

Net income: Euro 1.4 m;

- Tangible fixed assets to total balance sheet-ratio: 22.9%;
- Equity capital to total balance sheet-ratio: 27.4%;
- Return on equity capital (after taxes): 16.6%;
- Return on total capital (after taxes): 5.9%;
- Turnover: Euro 44.1 m;
- Net profit ratio (after taxes): 3.1%;
- Personnel expenditure: Euro 10.2 m;
- Personnel expenditure to turnover-ratio: 24.6%;
- Taxable income: Euro 2.2 m.

It has to be kept in mind that the above ratios are typical for the German manufacturing sector and therefore differ somewhat from the ratios used in other studies. For example, the weights for the sources of finance used in the other report prepared for the European Commission or in OECD (1991) and the Ruding Report (European Commission, 1992) are: retained earnings 55%, new equity 10% and debt 35%. The equivalent weights used here are: retained earnings 19% (6,513,453/34,914,854), new equity 9% (3,067,751/34,914,854) and debt 72% (25,333,650/34,914,854). Therefore only new equity carries approximately the same weight. When comparing the results of different studies these differing weights can explain varieties of effective tax burdens to a great extent.

The following lists the other important assumptions:

- Expected economic lifetimes for assets: production buildings (40 years); office buildings (50 years); patents and concessions (5 years each); plant and machinery (five assets are considered, 5 to 10 years); office furniture and fixtures (4 and 9 years); financial assets (all zero); stocks (zero).
- Rates of price increase: consumer price index (2.3%); price index for basic material (1.4%); price index for wages (2.5%); price index for investment goods (2.5%).
- Interest rates for creditors and debtors: short term credit (3%); long term credit (4.7%); short term debit (7%); long term debit (6%).

Shareholders and distributions: The base case example of a medium-sized company includes 10 shareholders (natural persons) who are located in the same country as the corporation (i.e. domestic shareholders). It is further assumed that all shareholders have identical pre-tax data such as participation rate (10%), family status (married) and number of children (1 child). The latter assumptions are relevant for the income tax tariff to be applied and for other personal allowances. The profit distributions (gross dividends) to the shareholders amount to Euro 511,290 (16% of the share capital) per period in each country. This means that each shareholder receives a gross dividend of Euro 51,129 per period. Moreover, the shareholders earn income from other sources (Euro 51,129 each per period) and receive interest on the loan granted to the corporation. The gross interest receipts amount to Euro 92,033 (6% of Euro 1,533,876) each period, i.e. each shareholder receives periodical interest income from loans of Euro 9,203.

Although the European Tax Analyzer takes only domestic investment into account the results provide some information for *economic distortions within the EU.* The relevant scenario concerns the location choice of individual companies. If we suppose that multinational investors ignore personal taxes of their shareholders, because they do not know the identity of the relevant (i.e. marginal) shareholder, and that the impact of the provisions far avoiding international double taxation leave effective tax rates close to those in the host country (where production takes place), the cross-country-comparison of the effective tax rates at the corporate level (ignoring personal taxes) reveals the relevant information as for the attractiveness of one location over another.

2 Comparison of the effective tax burden over a ten year period for a base case scenario assuming the tax regimes for the fiscal year 1999

2.1 Tax burden at the level of the corporation

2.1.1 Overview of results

The effective average tax rates (EATR) for the base case scenario, in which only the taxes at the level of the corporation are taken into account, are shown in Table 4.

Table 4: Effective average tax rate across 5 EU Member States and the USA - Only corporate taxes

	EATR		Difference to EU-5 Average	
	absolute in Euro	effective in %	absolute in %	effective in %
FRA	12,954,033	39.7	45.61	57.54
GER	11,290,464	32.8	26.91	30.16
IRL	3,504,761	8.3	-60.60	-67.06
NL	8,793,437	24.0	-1.15	-4.76
UK	7,937,863	21.0	-10.77	-16.67
EU-5 Average	8,896,112	25.2		
USA	10,480,517	29.7	17.81	17.86

There is a considerable variation in the EATR from 39.7% in France to 8.3% in Ireland resulting in a range of 31.4 percentage points. The average EATR of the 5 EU Member States (EU-5 in the following) is 25.2%. Only France and Germany are above the average, the remaining three countries are below the average figure. Whereas EATR in the Netherlands and the UK are similar to one another and to the average, the Irish tax burden is significantly lower.

The EATR of the US corporation ranges above the EU-5 average and is close to the one in Germany. Within the USA the number of taxes and thus the effective tax burden depends on the state in which a corporation is resident. In this report it is assumed that the corporation is located in California. The state of California is an important place of location for new technologies and industries. This, however, implies that besides the federal corporation tax an additional (franchise) tax on corporate income and a non-profit (property) tax at the state level have to be considered.

The differences between the EATR are always the result of the given input data of the company. Therefore they cannot be generalised. Moreover, these differences are caused by the national tax systems, taxes, tax bases and tax rates. These elements are explained below.

2.1.2 Impact of different taxes on the effective average tax burden

2.1.2.1 Overview

The following section examines the impact of the different taxes on the EATR in each country and the differences of the EATR between the countries. Since some taxes are deductible as business expenses from the bases of other taxes the interrelations between the various taxes have to be considered, in order to show this impact separately.[7] If a tax is deductible from the base of another tax, the effective burden of the first tax is lower compared to the nominal payment of this tax. The European Tax Analyzer can take these facts into account. Therefore, the model is run several times gradually eliminating those taxes that are deductible from the bases of other taxes. The effective burden of a tax is the difference between the EATR of subsequent simulations.

The results in Table 5 reveal that there is a considerable variation in the structure of the national tax systems. In all countries profit taxes have the highest impact on the EATR. The weights range, however, from 54.3% in France to 99.3% in Germany (including trade tax), the average of the EU-5 is 83.6% (including trade tax). The international comparison shows that the main cause of the comparatively high EATR in Germany is the level of profit taxation (corporation tax, solidarity levy on corporation tax and trade tax on corporate income). Compared to Germany, the burden of profit taxes is lower in all other countries. The differences, with reference to the EU-5 average are: Germany (+52.9%), USA (+32.6%), Netherlands (+18.2%), France (-4.0%) and the UK (-4.0%). The lowest burden with profit taxes is found in Ireland (-63.1%).

---

7 For example, real property tax can be deducted from the base of the corporation tax in all countries considered here.

Table 5: Impact of types of taxes on the effective average tax rate - Only corporate taxes

EATR - corporation	FRA	GER	IRL	NL	UK	EU-5 Average	USA
in Euro	12,954,033	11,290,464	3,504,761	8,793,437	7,937,863	8,896,112	10,480,517
Corporation tax and surcharges	7,037,881	8,689,994	2,704,136	8,659,264	7,033,418	6,824,939	8,392,151
Trade tax / franchise tax on income	-	2,517,630	-	-	-	503,526	1,327,614
Trade tax on capital / taxe profession-nelle	4,199,789	-	-	-	-	839,958	-
Employer's contribution	1,385,938	-	-	-	-	277,188	-
Property tax	-	-	-	-	-	-	760,752
Real property tax	330,425	82,840	800,625	134,173	904,445	450,501	-
relative in %	100.0	100.0	100.0	100.0	100.0	100.0	100.0
Corporation tax and surcharges	54.3	77.0	77.2	98.5	88.6	79.1	80.1
Trade tax / franchise tax on income	-	22.3	-	-	-	4.5	12.7
Trade tax on capital / taxe profession-nelle	32.4	-	-	-	-	6.5	-
Employer's contribution	10.7	-	-	-	-	2.1	-
Property tax	-	-	-	-	-	-	7.2
Real property tax	2.6	0.7	22.8	1.5	11.4	7.8	-

By contrast, the impact of non-profit taxes on the EATR is low on average. The only exception is France where the weight of the non-profit taxes amounts to 45.7%. This is caused by the high number of non-profit taxes. Whereas all other countries levy only one additional non-profit tax, there are three in France: real property tax, employer taxes and "taxe professionnelle" (business or trade tax). Compared with Germany this disadvantage more than compensates for the advantage of the lower profit tax burden in France.

2.1.2.2 Corporation tax

In all countries the corporation tax has by far the highest impact on the effective tax burden. However, there is a considerable variation among countries. In order to analyse the reasons for variations in more detail we have to distinguish between the tax base effects on the one hand and the tax rate effects on the other.

2.1.2.2.1 Tax bases (computation of taxable income)

The comparison of the corporation tax bases in Table 6 again reveals a large variation between the countries. If we take the EU-5 average as a benchmark the range between the maximum and the minimum in the EU is from +21.6% in Ireland to –50% in France. The US tax base is almost equal to EU-5 average (-0.8%). This considerable range is mainly caused by the low tax base in France.

Table 6: Comparison of overall corporation tax bases

	FRA	GER	IRL	NL	UK	EU-5 Average	USA
Average tax base in Euro	854,406	1,589,442	2,076,925	2,034,755	1,984,634	1,708,032	1,693,965
Difference to EU-5 - in Euro - in %	-853,627 -50.0	-118,590 -6.9	368,893 21.6	326,723 19.1	276,602 16.2		-14,068 -0.8

The differences between the corporation tax bases are lower than would be expected from the findings in many qualitative analyses of the tax bases. These differences are mainly caused by the different amounts of taxes deductible from the corporation tax base.[8] Moreover, as one would expect, taxable profits are influenced by depreciation practices, the deduction of pension costs and the

8 These are real property tax and trade tax in Germany, real property tax, employer taxes and "taxe professionnelle" in France, real property taxes (business rates) in Ireland, the Netherlands and the UK, and property tax and franchise tax on income in the USA.

valuation of stock (inventories). The differences between these important elements of the tax bases in the manufacturing sector are discussed in more detail now. Elements of the tax base of the model firm that have only a minor impact – for example, interest receipts or dividends from a participation in a subsidiary – are not considered. Table 7 shows the unweighted averages for the 10 calculation periods of the different elements.

Table 7: Comparison of different elements of corporation tax bases

	FRA	GER	IRL	NL	UK	EU-5 Average	USA
Depreciation overall	2, 599,984	2,537,167	2,366,471	2,378,803	2,305,100	2,437,505	2,493,830
Difference to EU-5							
- in Euro	162,479	99,662	-71,034	-58,702	-132,405	--	56,325
- in %	6.7	4.1	-2.9	-2.4	-5.4	--	2.3
Depreciation on buildings	163,204	139,889	93,260	99,920	93,260	117,907	110,911
Difference to EU-5							
- in Euro	45,298	21,983	-24,647	-17,986	-24,647	--	-6,996
- in %	32.4	15.7	-17.6	-12.9	-17.6	--	-5.0
Depreciation on tangible fixed assets	2,284,212	2,244,709	2,120,643	2,126,314	2,095,478	2,274,271	2,238,450
Difference to EU-5							
- in Euro	109,941	70,438	-53,628	-47,957	-78,794	--	64,178
- in %	5.1	3.2	-2.5	-2.2	-3.6	--	3.0
Depreciation on intangibles	152,568	152,568	152,568	152,568	116,363	145,327	144,469
Difference to EU-5							
- in Euro	7,241	7,241	7,241	7,241	-28,964	--	-858
- in %	5.0	5.0	5.0	5.0	-19.9	--	-0.6

Continuation Table 7:

	FRA	GER	IRL	NL	UK	EU-5 Average	USA
Pension costs (occupational scheme)	938,058	685,868	938,058	938,058	938,058	887,620	938,058
Difference to EU-5							
- in Euro	50,438	-201,752	50,438	50,438	50,438	--	50,438
- in %	5.7	-22.7	5.7	5.7	5.7	--	5.7
Company taxes deducted as business expenses	675,955	399,691	5,881	1,392	8,994	218,382	38,023
Difference to EU-5							
- in Euro	457,573	181,308	-212,501	-216,991	-209,389	--	-180,359
- in %	209.5	83.0	-97.3	-99.4	-95.9	--	-82.6
Production costs of goods sold	38,861,264	34,535,977	39,257,820	39,212,851	39,233,716	38,220,326	39,486,659
Difference to EU-5							
- in Euro	640,938	-3,684,349	1,037,495	992,526	1,013,390	--	1,266,333
- in %	1.7	-9.6	2.7	2.6	2.7	--	3.3

2.1.2.2.1.1 Depreciation

In the countries considered here the overall amount of depreciation that can be deducted from the tax base by the model-firm is highest in France, closely followed by Germany. Both countries range above EU-5 average (France 6.7% and Germany 4.1%). The other Member States may only depreciate less than EU-5 average with the UK in the last position (-5.4%). Depreciation in the USA is a little above EU-5 average (2.3%). Depreciation on buildings, tangible fixed assets and intangibles must be distinguished from one another.

Depreciation of buildings: In all countries buildings are depreciated according to the straight-line method. Deviations between the amounts of depreciation result from different depreciation periods. Due to the short period of 20 years depreciation of buildings is highest in France. The periods in the other countries are: 25 years in Germany, Ireland and the UK, 35 years in the Netherlands and 39 years in the USA. The reason for the comparatively low amounts of depreciation in Ireland and the UK is that office buildings may not be depreciated.

Depreciation of tangible fixed assets: The differences between depreciation of these assets (plant and machinery, furniture and fixtures) shown in Table 7 are caused by different methods and rates of depreciation. If allowed, the depreciation of fixed assets that belong to the model-firm is based on the national declining-balance methods. Again, within the EU, only France (5.1%) and Germany (3.2%) range above average. The comparatively high amounts of depreciation in France are the result of the depreciation rates. Depending on the period of use they can rise up to 50% whereas the maximum in Germany is fixed to 30%. Although there is no such strict limitation of the depreciation rates in the USA the deductible amounts are lower because of the half year convention. This rule limits the depreciation in the year of acquisition to 50% of the annual depreciation. The amounts of depreciation in Ireland, the UK and the Netherlands are below EU-5 average. Whereas in the UK this can be attributed to the limitation of the depreciation rate of the declining-balance method to 25% and the prohibition on switching from the declining-balance to straight line in order to arrive at 100% depreciation, Ireland and, in general, the Netherlands apply only the straight-line method.

Depreciation of intangibles: With respect to intangibles, companies located in the UK and the USA can deduct less depreciation compared with the other countries, all at which apply the straight-line method. There are different reasons for these deviations: The UK operates the same 25% declining-balance pool method as for fixed assets and disallows switching to the straight line method. The USA prescribe the half year convention.

2.1.2.2.1.2 **Pension costs**

The rules of the national tax codes for the deductibility of pension costs are rather complex. In principle, the deductibility depends on the manner in which the occupational pension scheme is financed. With respect to the financing, we can distinguish between funded and unfunded schemes.[9] Funded schemes prevail in the Anglo-Saxon countries (Ireland, UK, USA) as well as in France and the Netherlands. In these countries companies make regular cash contributions to a pension fund (or an insurance company) which collects the money and is responsible for the future pension payments to the employees. The predominant system in Germany[10] is an unfunded scheme. This differs from a funded scheme with respect to the person legally responsible for the future pension payments. In

---

9 Sometimes we can also find a distinction between trust concepts (which are funded schemes) and direct financing (which is an unfunded scheme). See Kvist (1992: 6).

10 Funded schemes are also present and are gaining popularity in Germany. See Arbeitskreis "Betriebliche Pensionsfonds" (1998).

an unfunded scheme the company (employer) is responsible, whereas in the case of a funded scheme the pension fund (or the insurance company) is responsible. In both cases, however, the costs for the future pension payments are deductible from the tax base of the company (employer) upon realisation: in the case of a funded scheme the premiums paid to the pension fund are deductible and in the case of an unfunded scheme the company accounts for a pension reserve in the balance sheet and deducts annual contributions to this book reserve from the tax base.

From an economic point of view, the pension liability and premiums in the case of a pension fund on the one hand and the book reserve for pensions and contributions to this reserve on the other hand express the same thing: they show the annual and the accumulated pension costs. A meaningful comparison of the tax effects of pension costs has to include both methods of financing future pensions and consider, as a starting point, equivalent pension obligations.

The base case considers a defined benefit pension plan, taking the projected final salary of each employee as a basis.[11] Since we assume an identical pension plan in each country, the *total pension costs* that are deductible from the company's tax base over the professional life of an employee do not differ between the countries. However, what may differ, are the *average pension costs* eligible for deduction in a certain period. From the results in Table 7 we can see that the deductible amount in Germany is lower than in all other countries. For the purposes of simplification we have assumed identical rules for the calculation of the contributions to a pension fund in the other countries. They are based on international accounting standards following the US-GAAP (Generally Accepted Accounting Principles). The relatively disadvantageous position of the German corporation can be attributed to three reasons:

- *Actuarial assumptions*: The valuation of the liabilities of a pension plan and, hence the annual amount of the contributions to either a pension fund or a book reserve, are based on actuarial assumptions that apply a certain discount rate. Whereas in Germany this discount factor is fixed in the income tax code (para 6a EStG) at a rate of currently 6%, it is derived from the market interest rate (or government bonds) in the other countries. At the moment a rate of 5% is applied. The higher German discount rate implies, however, lower *periodical contributions* and thus lower deductible *average pension costs* in the early years of an individual pension agreement leaving the *total pension costs* unchanged.

Accounting standards: It is assumed that the future pension payments are based on the final salary of an employee. In order to evaluate the pension liability accordingly, a steady increase in salary due to the increase of labour costs has to be taken into account. In contrast to the situation in Germany where the value is

---

11 The model-firm employs 268 persons with an average age of 47 years. The retirement age is fixed at 65.

based on the prices on the reporting date and take into account only price increases since the prior reporting date, the international valuation standards of pension funds allow a projection of future price increase. Due to this projection, the amount of deductible *average pension costs* is higher in the other countries in the early years of an individual pension agreement.

- *Other restrictions in the tax codes*: In contrast to the situation in the other countries it is forbidden in Germany to deduct contributions for employees who are less than 30 years old. This again results in lower *average pension costs*.

Altogether, the deductible *average pension costs* are around 37% lower in Germany than in the other countries. This result is confirmed by empirical surveys (see Küting and Strickmann, 1997: 10) and previous studies (see Klein, 1990: 133). One has to be aware, however, that this result cannot be generalised as it is sensitive to the assumptions made for the pension plan. If we assumed a defined contribution plan instead of a defined benefit plan, or something different from a final salary scheme, Germany's disadvantage would be reduced. Moreover, an increase of the market interest rate and thus the assumed discount rate of a pension fund would also reduce Germany's disadvantage.

Contributions to a pension reserve differ from contributions to a pension fund with respect to the cash flow effects. Whereas in case of a pension reserve the cash flow of a company is only affected by the future pension payments (i.e. the contributions and thus the deductible pension costs do not affect the cash flow), the contributions to a pension fund reduce the cash flow far before the pensions are paid out to the employees. A pension reserve therefore seems to offer advantages for the self-financing of a company with respect to the liquidity effects. However, these advantages are very limited if we consider that the company could use the additional liquidity to decrease long term loans (capital substitution). Since pension reserves have to be discounted, the advantage is limited to the difference between the market interest rate and the discount rate. If we compare current market interest rates with the fixed discount rate for pension reserves in Germany of 6%, there is presumably no great effect. The principle aim of the European Tax Analyzer is to show the tax consequences of different (accounting) options in isolation. Therefore, instead of capital substitution, it is assumed that a company which is building up a pension reserve puts the additional liquidity into an internal fund and invests the money on the capital market (asset funding or capital accumulation). This accumulated capital together with the (taxable) interest resulting from the investment of the money (the money could be invested in, e.g., securities) serves to fund the future pension payments.

Compared to the use of a pension fund, asset funding or capital accumulation has the same periodical effects on the free cash flow of the company. Therefore, the occupational pension schemes have no consequences beyond the tax effects shown in Table 7. It should be emphasised that the above assumptions are not only of a theoretical nature. There is a large and growing body of empirical relevance regarding the value of asset funding in Germany.[12]

2.1.2.2.1.3 Company taxes deducted as business expenses

The differences between the corporation tax bases can be attributed to a great extent to the numbers and amounts of deductible taxes. In Germany (real property tax and trade tax) and particularly in France (real property tax, employer taxes and "taxe professionnelle") the deductible taxes are far above EU-5 average. By contrast, the relatively insignificant amounts in Ireland (real property tax), the Netherlands (real property tax), the United Kingdom (real property tax) and the United States (property tax and franchise tax on income) result in deductible taxes far below EU-5 average.

Table 8: Comparison of overall corporation tax bases without deductible taxes

	FRA	GER	IRL	NL	UK	EU-5 Average	USA
Average tax base in Euro	1,530,361	1,989,133	2,082,806	2,036,146	1,993,627	1,926,415	1,731,988
Difference to EU-5							
- in Euro	-396,054	62,718	156,391	109,732	67,213		-194,427
- in %	-20.6	3.3	8.1	5.7	3.5		-10.1

If we refrained from the deduction of these taxes, the differences between the corporation tax bases would be reduced considerably. Table 8 shows that, compared to the base case, the span from the highest to the lowest tax base with reference to the EU-5 average would decrease from 71.6 (-50.0% in France and 21.6% in Ireland) presented in Table 6 to 28.7 percentage points (-20.6% in France and 8.1% in Ireland).

2.1.2.2.1.4 Production costs and inventory valuation

Another important reason for the variation in the corporation tax base is the difference in the rules for the valuation of stock (inventories). In the base case, the *production costs* for the finished goods or work in process are valued at variable costs in Germany and France and at full costs in all other countries. The production costs calculated according to the national accounting standards and

---

12 See Deutsche Bank Research (1995). Similar effects on the cash flow would be obtained in case of a reinsurance contract.

taking into account available valuation options are by far lowest in Germany. The most important reason for this is that the production costs for finished goods and work in progress must include an appropriate allocation of administration expenses in the manufacturing overheads in all countries except Germany. Germany grants a specific valuation option which the model firm has exercised in the interest of tax minimisation. Moreover, the amount of taxes that are part of the production costs (e.g. local taxes like real property tax) is lowest in Germany.

The extent to which these differences between the production costs affect the (balance sheet) value of the inventories depends on the *allocation method for inventories* (e.g. average cost method, FIFO or LIFO) applied in each country and the storage period.[13] We have assumed FIFO in Ireland, the Netherlands, the UK and the USA and average cost method in France and Germany as standard allocation methods. We have further assumed a small periodical increase in the stock (i.e. production exceeds sales). Under these assumptions the value of the inventories and the value of the production costs of the goods sold, which is deducted from the tax base, are by far lowest in Germany. Compared to the EU-5 average shown in Table 7, the difference amounts to almost –9.6%. The other countries are all above the EU-5 average (between 1.7% in France and 2.7% in Ireland and the UK). The highest value can be found in the USA (3.3% above the EU-5 average). The low value of production costs in Germany means, however, that certain elements that do not have to be included (e.g. parts of depreciation, personal expenses, pension costs) can be set against taxable income earlier than in the other countries. In fact, all costs that are not included in the production costs can be deducted immediately from the corporation tax base. This also means that from a point of view of a German corporation, the disadvantage over France with respect to depreciation and the disadvantage over all other countries (including France) with respect to pension costs is reduced to a certain extent. It always has to be kept in mind that this effect, like all other differences between the corporation tax bases described above, is only temporary. The result of this timing difference is an interest gain.

2.1.2.2.2 Tax rates

The other element that has an impact on the corporation tax burden is the tax rate. The corporation tax rate on undistributed income is highest in Germany at 40%. Except Ireland, with its manufacturing relief of 10%, the other four countries are all roughly at the level of 1/3 (see Table 9). There are also different tax rate structures: while there is a proportional rate in France, Germany, Ireland and the Netherlands, the tax rate in the UK and the USA differ with respect to 2 (UK) or 8 (USA) income brackets. Moreover, there are currently temporary corporation tax surcharges in France (20%) and Germany (5.5%) resulting in a statutory

---

13 If all goods that were produced were sold in the same period the storage period is zero and there would be no difference between the different allocation methods.

corporation tax rate of 40% (France) and 42.2% (Germany) respectively. Both tax rates are by far highest among the EU-5.[14]

Table 9: Statutory corporation tax rate including surcharges

	FRA	GER	IRL	NL	UK	EU-5 Average	USA
Corporation tax rate	33.33%	40%	10%	35%	20-30%	27.7-29.7%	15-39% (marginal 35%)
Surcharges	20%	5.5%	-	-	-	5.1%	-
Corporation tax rate including surcharges	40%	42.2%	10%	35%	20-30%	29.4-31.4%	15-39%

Especially from the point of view of a German corporation, this tax rate differential more than compensates for the lower German tax base compared with all other countries. The consequences for a French corporation are similar but less severe. Despite having the highest corporation tax base Ireland benefits greatly from its very low tax rate, which results in by far the lowest effective corporation tax burden among EU-5 countries (see Table 10). In numerical terms and with reference to the EU-5 average as a benchmark, Ireland is the only country with an effective corporation tax burden below the EU-5 average (-60.4%). The other countries are all above the EU-5 average (France +3.1%, UK +3.1%, the Netherlands +26.9%, Germany +27.3% and the USA +23%).

14 The different "contributions" in France were introduced in 1995 and the solidarity levy in Germany has been in place since 1991. However, the level of these surcharges has changed during these periods.

Table 10: Statutory corporation tax rate including surcharges, corporation tax base and effective burden with corporation tax

	FRA	GER	IRL	NL	UK	EU-5 Average	USA
Corporation tax rate[a)]	40%	42.2%	10%	35%	30%	31.4%	35%
(Ranking)	(4)	(5)	(1)	(3)	(2)		
Corporation tax base[b)]	854,406	1,589,442	2,076,925	2,034,755	1,984,634	1,708,032	1,693,965
(Ranking)	(1)	(2)	(5)	(4)	(3)		
Corporation tax burden[c)]	7,037,881	8,689,994	2,704,136	8,659,264	7,033,418	6,824,939	8,392,151
(Ranking)	(3)	(5)	(1)	(4)	(2)		
a) See Table 9; b) Average per period, see Table 6; c) Over 10 year simulation period, see Table 5							

Altogether, with a little exception for France and the Netherlands, the ranking of the countries with respect to the effective burden with corporation tax closely follows the country-ranking with respect to the tax rates (see Table 10). This means that the effective burden with corporation tax is influenced above all by the tax rate. The impact of the tax base in general is only minor.

2.1.2.3 Trade tax on income and other taxes on corporate income

Germany levies a trade tax on income as well as the corporation tax and its solidarity levy. The trade tax on income is based on the same taxable profits computed for the corporation tax, which has to be modified by certain additions and reductions. In particular, one half of the interest payments on long-term debt is added back to the taxable profit. The effective tax rate set by the municipalities for the year 1999 is on average 17.56%.[15] There is no comparable second or third tax on income in France, Ireland, the Netherlands and the UK, but US States can levy their own "franchise tax on income" or state corporation tax. The State of California where the model firm is located, levies such a franchise tax. Like the German trade tax, the franchise tax on income in California is an additional tax on profits. The basis of assessment is similar to that used for the US-federal corporation tax, but with fewer modifications than in Germany. In particular,

15 This is based on an average local tax coefficient ("Hebesatz") of 426%.

interest expenses are fully deductible and therefore the tax base tends to be lower than for the trade tax on income in Germany. However, at the same time this results in a more distinct discrimination against equity financing than in Germany. Moreover, the German tax rate (17.56%) is higher than in the USA (8.8%) so that the total local income tax burden in Germany exceeds the corresponding US burden by around 90%.

Taking the additional local taxes on corporate income in Germany and the USA into account and with reference to the EU-5 average as a benchmark, the effective overall burden on corporate income is by far highest in Germany. Germany (+52.9%) and the Netherlands (+18.2%) are the only Member States ranking above EU-5 average. The position of the US corporation in the country ranking is also above the average (+32.6%). The corresponding tax burdens in France (-4.0%), the UK (-4.0%) and especially in Ireland (-63.1%) are lower.[16]

2.1.2.4 Non profit taxes

2.1.2.4.1 Real property tax (real estate tax)

France, Germany, Ireland, the Netherlands and the UK all levy an annual tax on real estate under specific rules. The capital invested in land and buildings is also subject to annual taxation in the USA, but within the scope of the general property tax discussed below.

The structure of the real property or real estate tax differs greatly among countries. Whereas France (27.2%), Ireland (63%) and the UK (47.4%) levy high tax rates on a comparably low tax base, the situation in the two other countries is different. In Germany (1.5% assuming an average tax coefficient ("Hebesatz") of 444%) and in the Netherlands (0.4%) broader tax bases are combined with lower tax rates. The tax rates are set by the municipalities in each country and should represent a country average. The higher basis of assessment in Germany and the Netherlands can be attributed to the fact that both countries base their assessment on the "current value" whereas, in the other three countries, the basis is derived from the net annual rental value of the property.

Altogether, real property tax is lowest in Germany and highest in the UK. Compared with the EU-5 average the following differences can be calculated: Germany (-81.6%), Netherlands (-70.2%), France (-26.7%), Ireland (+77.7%) and the UK (+100.8%).[17] It is only in Ireland and the UK where the real property tax (so-called rates) represent a significant cost of doing business. Their portions in

---

[16] These figures are derived from Table 5.

[17] The figures are taken from Table 5.

the overall average tax burden amount to 22.8% in Ireland[18] and 11.4% in the UK. In both countries, as in the Netherlands, real property tax is the only tax in addition to corporation tax.

2.1.2.4.2 Property taxes

Other than Luxembourg, no Member State of the EU imposes a general property tax on the value of the assets of a corporation. Of the Member States considered here, Germany has levied a property tax but it was abolished in 1997.

In the USA, non-profit taxes are not imposed on the federal level. The States (e.g. California), however, may levy property taxes. Almost all assets (including land and buildings) except intangibles and inventories are incorporated in the tax base. Since debts are not deductible from the base, property tax in general does not discriminate against different forms of financing a corporation. The valuation rules differ between movable and immovable property: while the valuation of immovable property is (in general) based on a cost basis, movable property is assessed at market or fair cash values. The tax rates vary between 0.06% and 3%; the tax rate of the State of California is 1%. The portion of the property tax in the average effective tax burden of a US corporation amounts to 7.2% (see Table 5).

2.1.2.4.3 Other non-profit taxes

France is the only country with other significant non-profit taxes. There are "taxe professionnelle" and employers' taxes. The latter cover three smaller taxes: apprentice tax ("taxe d'apprentissage"), the professional training levy ("participation des employeurs à la formation professionnelle continue") and the housing levy ("participation des employeurs à l'effort de construction"). The base of the "taxe professionnelle" comprises tangible fixed assets, land and buildings and 18% of the payroll. Tangible fixed assets are valued at 16% of their historical acquisition costs, for land and building twice of the base of the real property tax is used. Since the taxable assets are valued under a standardised system, their age, and therefore depreciation is not taken into account. Besides a general deduction of 16%, there is no allowance for further deductions (e.g. debts). Tax rates are set by the French municipalities and can therefore vary across the country. The average tax rate in 1999 was 23.2%. The total payroll of a French corporation is further subject to employers' taxes, the nominal burden of which amounts to 2.45% of the payroll. Consequently, the total nominal burden of the payroll in France due to "taxe professionnelle" and employers' taxes is around 5.8%.

---

18 Besides the high nominal burden of real property tax in Ireland the high figure results from the low corporation tax rate in Ireland which limits the tax savings due to deductibility from the tax base.

As a result of the high portion of non-profit taxes the structure of the French tax system differs significantly from the other countries. "Taxe professionnelle" and employers' taxes burden capital- and labour-intensive companies in particular. Together, both taxes have a significant impact on the effective average tax burden of a French company. In this model, "taxe professionnelle" accounts for 32% and employers' taxes for 11% of the effective average tax burden of the French corporation (see Table 5).

2.2 Tax burden at the overall level (corporation and domestic shareholders)

2.2.1 Relevance of shareholder taxation (personal taxes)

The academic literature provides no clear answer to the question whether the personal taxes of the shareholders on dividends and other forms of capital income should be included in an international comparison of the effective tax burdens of companies. Given the assumption that companies always act in the interests of their owners (i.e. their shareholders), the answer is certainly yes.

In practise, however, difficulties arise when accounting for personal taxes. These difficulties seem to depend to a great extent on the size of a company. If we first consider a *multinational company* with many shareholders, it is often argued that for the decision making purposes only taxes paid by the company are taken into account. This is explained by the fact that multinational companies have many different tax-paying and tax-exempt shareholders which could be resident or non-resident individuals and separate legal entities respectively. Since it is not easy and sometimes even impossible to identify the relevant shareholders and their tax position it is reasonable to conclude that personal taxes do not matter. Therefore personal taxes are often excluded from an international comparison of the effective tax burdens of companies.[19] It should be pointed out, however, that this is merely a simplifying assumption. A closer look at the information provided about shareholders in the annual reports of multinational companies reveals that multinationals know more about the personal status and residence than one might expect. Therefore, like for the types of investment, several categories of shareholders could be included in the comparison in order to overcome this uncertainty. However, in certain situations not accounting for personal taxes may

---

19 Excluding personal taxes does not mean, however, that the tax burden can be interpreted as the one facing a tax-exempt shareholder. The reason is that the tax treatment of tax-exempt shareholders might differ in different tax jurisdictions. For example it is not clear whether under an imputation system all kinds of tax-exempt shareholders can claim an imputation credit.

be justified. If we consider the decision of a multinational company regarding the location of a – in general fully owned – subsidiary, the taxes borne by the subsidiary in the host country are of primary concern. Personal taxes in the host country of the subsidiary do not matter because there are no other shareholders besides the parent company. We could even leave out taxation at the level of the parent company if foreign source income is taxed without regard to the host country of the subsidiary. This is quite a common situation. Moreover, even the personal taxes of the shareholders of the parent company in the home country do not seem to matter because there is only additional income (and sometimes non-profit) taxation on the distributed profits of the parent company irrespective of the origin of the income.

However, the situation is different if we consider *small and medium-sized companies* (SMEs). Since these companies maintain close relations to their (managing) owners, they know the tax status of their shareholders. Moreover, as the access of SMEs to the international capital markets is limited, and the most important source of income for the owners is the company and its profits respectively, the amount of the profits after personal taxes is relevant for the financing of the company. In cases where personal taxes and their interaction with corporate taxes are relevant, a comparison of the effective levels of company taxation should also include different tax planning opportunities concerning the financing of a company by its shareholders with debt or equity.

2.2.2 Comparison and analysis of results

This study of the effective levels of company taxation focuses on domestic investment and considers as a base case model firm a typical manufacturing *medium-sized company*. Therefore, the taxation of the shareholders and thus the effective overall tax burden is computed in a separate step. The base case includes 10 identical shareholders who are resident in the same country as the corporation.[20] The overall effective average tax burden over a ten year period including personal taxes is shown in Table 11.

Compared to the tax burden at the level of the corporation (see Table 4 above), the overall tax burden including personal taxes is rising. Within the EU-5[21], there is no change in the country ranking: France still has the highest (48.8%) and Ireland[22] the lowest EATR (17.2%). However, there is considerable variation between the effective levels of shareholder taxation (see Table 11). France is still on top, but now we see the Netherlands in fourth and Ireland in third position

---

20 The assumptions about the shareholders are summarised in section 1.4.

21 The USA is closing in and is almost equal to the Netherlands.

22 If we did not consider manufacturing relief in Ireland and applied the 28% corporation tax rate instead, Ireland (28.1%) and the UK (25.6%) would change their places in the country ranking. See Table B2 of Appendix B for the results.

whereas Germany improves to second and the UK to the first position within the EU. US shareholders bear the lowest tax burden.[23]

Table 11: Effective average tax rate across 5 EU Member States and the USA - Corporate and personal taxes

	EATR shareholder	EATR overall (corporation and shareholder)		Difference to EU-Average	
	absolute in Euro	absolute in Euro	effective in %	absolute in %	effective in %
FRA	5,664,355	18,618,388	48.8	37.76	51.55
GER	4,249,136	15,539,600	37.4	14.98	16.15
IRL	4,697,939	8,202,700	17.2	-39.31	-46.58
NL	4,955,073	13,748,510	32.0	1.72	-0.62
UK	3,530,026	11,467,888	25.6	-15.15	-20.50
EU-5 Average	4,619,305	13,515,417	32.2		
USA	3,306,954	13,787,471	32.0	2.01	-0.62

Ultimately, besides corporate taxes, the differences at the overall level come from the interaction of corporate and personal income taxes (i.e. the corporation tax system), the individual income tax rates including surcharges and capital taxes at the shareholder level.

2.2.2.1 *Corporation tax systems*

Germany completely avoids double taxation of domestic dividends by crediting the corporation tax borne by the company in full against the ultimate income tax liability of the shareholder.[24] The French corporation tax system, like the German system, is an imputation system. However, economic double taxation of dividends is not entirely eliminated. Due to the surcharges on the corporation tax rate and the limitation of the tax credit (avoir fiscal) to one half of the distributed dividend, only 75% of the underlying corporation tax are credited against personal income tax. Although there is no imputation system, the situation in the Netherlands is quite similar. Instead of a tax credit, qualified shareholders (a participation rate of

23 What is interesting to note is that in Ireland the shareholders pay more taxes (4,697,939 Euro) than the corporation (3,504,761 Euro).

24 However, trade tax on corporate income is not credited against personal income tax in Germany. For the solidarity levy, a simplified imputation system applies.

at least 5% is required which is fulfilled in our base case which considers 10 shareholders and thus a participation rate of 10%) are entitled to a shareholder relief, which grants a lower income tax rate on dividends (25%) instead of the statutory income tax rate (marginal rate of 60%). Since 1999, the UK also applies a shareholder relief system. On the one hand, dividends carry a tax credit of 10% which is, however, not refunded. On the other hand the top income tax rate for dividends is now lower (32.5%) than the ordinary top income tax rate (40%). Altogether, for top rate shareholders the tax credit and the reduced income tax rate means that about 58% of the underlying corporation tax is credited against personal income tax. In Ireland and the USA there is no tax credit or relief at all (classical system). To the extent that the tax credit or relief is denied or restricted, the corporation tax represents a final burden, which tends to make dividend distributions less attractive than they would be in a full imputation system.

2.2.2.2 Income tax rates

Income tax burdens below EU-5 average can be found in three countries:[25] Germany (-5.9%), the UK (-21.8%) and the USA (-27.9%). By contrast, three countries rank above the average: France (23.1%), Ireland (4.1%) and the Netherlands (0.5%). As the model assumes an identical pre-tax income for all shareholders, theses differences can be attributed to the average income tax rates. The average income tax rate expresses the relation of the income tax due to taxable income. In the following the income tax rates and the taxable income when they apply are examined.

Of the six countries that are under review, France has the highest income tax burden. This can be attributed to the highest marginal rate (61.25% including several surcharges on income tax (prélèvements fiscaux) beginning at a taxable income of Euro 44,760). France is followed by Ireland which has a marginal income tax rate of 46% beginning with a taxable income of Euro 12,698. In the Netherlands, shareholder relief of 25% is granted exclusively for dividend income, whereas income from all other sources (e.g. interest income) is fully taxed at a rate of 60% starting at a taxable income of Euro 48,080. The marginal income tax rate in Germany is around 58% including supplementary levies such as the solidarity levy and church tax. Although the marginal rate is higher than in Ireland, the German income tax burden is lower because the marginal rate does not start below a taxable income of Euro 61,376. Income tax burdens and marginal income tax rates are lowest in the UK and the USA. In the UK the marginal rate is 40% (32.5% for dividends) starting at a taxable income of Euro 44,288. The marginal rate is 45.2% in the USA and starts at a taxable income of Euro 326,210.[26]

---

25 See Table B2 of Appendix B for detailed data.

26 The US income tax comprises federal income tax (39.6%) and income tax of the State of California (9.6%) Federal income tax can be deducted from State's income tax.

2.2.2.3 Capital taxes

France and the Netherlands charge the total assets including the value of shares in companies to annual property taxes at marginal rates of 1.8% (France) and 0.7% (Netherlands) respectively. With respect to the value of shares of a corporation, the marginal rate is reduced to zero (France) and 0,224% (Netherlands) in the case of a qualified participation. The USA (e.g. the State of California) also levies a property tax but exempts the value of shares from the tax base. Germany (since 1997), Ireland and the UK do not levy any net asset or similar form of capital tax.

Altogether, the results show that for the assumptions of the base case, the average effective tax burden at the overall level, is above all influenced by the different levels of company taxes in the countries under review. The country ranking at the corporation level and the overall level are the same. Due to differences between the corporation tax systems, the income tax rates and the structure of the capital taxes, it seems reasonable to conclude, that the results depend on the assumptions about the relevant economic data and therefore cannot be generalised. In order to obtain more universally valid results, sensitivity analysis is necessary. This will be done in section 3.3 below.

2.3 Conclusions

The main aim of this section was to compare the effective average tax rates (EATR) between corporations in five EU Member States (France, Germany, Ireland, Netherlands, UK) and the USA. The base case considered a medium-sized corporation with economic data that is typical for the manufacturing sector. The personal taxes of the shareholders were included in a separate step.

With respect to the tax burden at the *level of the corporation* the results revealed a considerable range of the EATR from 39.7% in France to 8.3% in Ireland. This result indicates considerable economic distortions within the EU with respect to companies which compete on the same market. The average EATR of the EU Member States is 25.2%; the EATR of the US corporation is above this average and amounts to 29.7%.

The corporation tax has by far the highest impact on the EATR. Although there is a large variation between the domestic corporation tax bases, the ranking of the countries with respect to the effective tax burden closely follows the level of the statutory tax rates. Since there exist no considerable non-profit taxes, in general, it therefore seems reasonable to conclude that the profit taxes have by far the highest impact on the effective tax burden. The only exception is France with a high portion of non-profit taxes. This is also the reason why the structure of the French tax system differs significantly from the other countries.

Finally, if *personal taxes* are also *included*, the range of the EATR becomes even higher. This suggests that there is more variation in personal taxes than in corporate taxes. Besides the level of corporate taxes, the differences in the presence of personal taxes can be attributed to corporation tax systems, the average income tax rates and the levy of capital taxes. However, the country ranking with reference to the EATR is the same as at the level of corporation.

3 Sensitivity analysis

3.1 Primary remarks

Since the effective average tax burden depends on the concrete economic data of a corporation and their shareholders, differences between the structures of the national tax systems can

- on the one hand distort competition in the European Union (EU) and
- on the other hand influence decisions of companies such as location, investment, financing, dividend policies etc.

Box 1: Classification of sensitivity analysis

A. Only corporate taxes

1. Investment. Tangible fixed assets to total balance sheet ratio.
2. Financing. Equity to total capital ratio.
3. Profitability. Pre tax return.
4. Industry. Specific company data for different industries.

B. Corporate and personal taxes

5. Dividend policies. Rate of distribution.
6. Financing. Equity to total capital ratio.

In order to test the robustness of the results based on the economic assumptions of the base case, the effects of alternative assumptions of the input data on the EATR are analysed by using „what-if“ or sensitivity analysis. The sensitivity analysis covers data both at the level of the corporation and the level of the shareholders shown in Box 1.

3.2 Level of the corporation

3.2.1 Investment policy

We vary the tangible fixed assets to total balance sheet ratio of the model firm in order to make the impact of the structure of the types of assets on the EATR clear. In so doing the quantity of tangible fixed assets as a percentage of total assets (i.e. balance sheet total) compared with the base case data is raised or reduced by 10% or 20% respectively. In other words, this variation takes into account a change in the model firm's capital intensity. The ratio in the base case is 22.9%. In order to keep the total balance sheet constant, the value for the financial assets was reduced or raised accordingly. Moreover, in order to isolate the effect of the modified investment policy, both the turnover and the interest receipts remain unchanged.

Figure 1: Effective average tax rate across 5 EU Member States and the USA
- Variation of tangible fixed assets to total balance sheet ratio
- Only corporate taxes

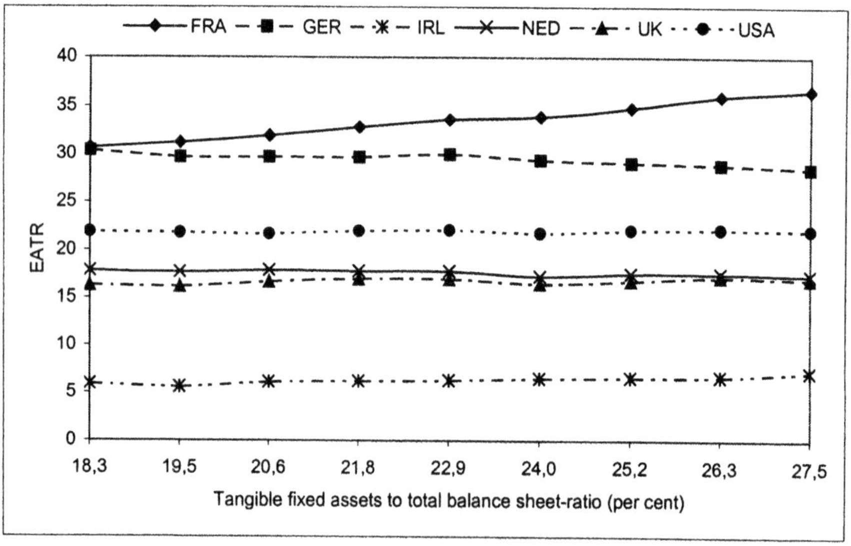

The results in Figure 1 show that, with the exception of Germany and the Netherlands, the EATR increases with the capital intensity.

Thus, only the situations in Germany and the Netherlands show the expected result: due to a shift from less generous rules for non-depreciable assets (i.e. financial assets) to a more generous capital allowance practice for depreciable assets (i.e. tangible fixed assets) the EATR decreases with the capital intensity. The EATR increase in the other countries is due to the levy of non-profit taxes.

- In the case of Ireland, the UK and the USA, it is above all the higher level of real property tax (property tax in the USA) in the overall tax burden that overcompensates for the effects of the capital allowances and is therefore decisive in causing the increase. However, the EATR increases are only minor.
- In contrast to the situation in Ireland, the UK and the USA, the EATR increase in France is noticeable. This can be attributed to the structure of the French „taxe professionnelle“. The base of the „taxe professionnelle“ includes tangible fixed assets but exempts intangibles and financial assets. Therefore, although the capital intensity is rising, the higher portion of tangible fixed assets in the tax bases is not compensated for by a lower portion of financial assets because these assets are exempt from non-profit taxation.

It seems reasonable to conclude from the results that capital-intensive production is discriminated in all countries except Germany and the Netherlands. The reason for this distortion of investment decisions is the levy of non-profit taxes or more precisely the absence of tax bases that include all of the relevant types of assets and of uniform rules for the evaluation of the assets. Although there are no changes in the countries' EATR-ranking, France and Germany are very similar in case of a low capital intensity.

3.2.2 Structure of finance

The aim of this section is to investigate the impact of changing assumptions regarding corporate financing on the EATR. Therefore, the weighting of the sources of financing is gradually changed by increasing the equity to total capital ratio from 25% to 100%. This increase is accompanied by a reduction of the interest expenses for long term debts. The other data does not change.

From the results shown in Figure 2 we can see that the EATR increases with the equity to total capital ratio in all countries. Therefore, the national tax systems are not neutral towards the source of company finance. The most important reason for this result is the effect of the corporation tax. While interest expenses are deductible from taxable profits, dividends must be paid out of profits upon which taxes have been paid. Thus, the more a company is financed by equity capital, the greater the corporation tax burden.

The discrimination against equity financing at the level of the corporation is most evident in Germany and the USA. Besides the high level of corporation tax rate, this result is caused by the levy of other taxes that do not treat the payments for debt and equity capital equally. On the one hand, in Germany interest expenses for long term debt can be deducted to the extent of one half from the base of the trade tax on income. Interest expenses in the USA are fully deductible even from the base of the franchise tax on income levied by the states. On the other hand, there are no reductions in the relevant tax bases for dividends paid to the shareholders. Therefore, the EATR in both countries increases disproportionately to the equity to total capital ratio.

Figure 2: Effective average tax rate across 5 EU Member States and the USA
- Variation of equity to total capital ratio
- Only corporate taxes

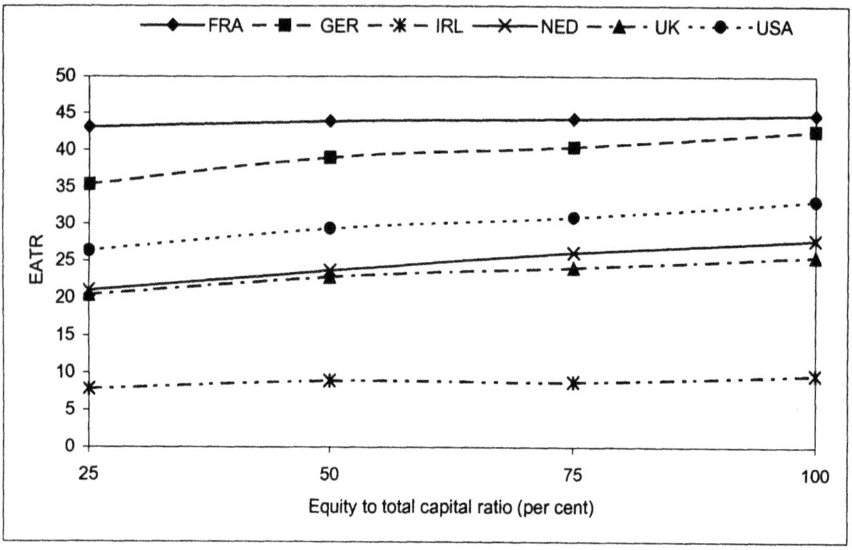

By contrast, the increase of the EATR is lower by far in Ireland and the UK. Since both countries apply the lowest corporation tax rate and levy no other taxes that discriminate against a certain source of finance, the reduction or saving of taxes due to the deductibility of interest is also lowest.

Altogether the results show that the EATR rises with an increasing equity to total capital ratio. However, since the discrimination against equity financing in contrast to debt financing is common in all tax systems that are under review, the EATRs neither cross nor converge. Therefore, differing assumptions about the debt to equity ratio do not change the country ranking of our base case. The level of variation within the sources of finance depends to a great extent on the level of the statutory corporation tax rate. With reference to Ireland and the UK, low tax rates tend to reduce such variations. Whether the increasing EATR is definitely proof tax driven discrimination against equity financing cannot be stated for certain. The answer depends on whether one considers the inclusion of personal taxes and thus, the taxation of dividends and interest income in the hands of the shareholders to be relevant or not. Therefore, personal taxes will be included in a separate step (see Chapter III 2 below).

3.2.3 Profitability

The EATR also depends on the assumed value for the pre-tax return of the company. There are at least two reasons for this dependence:

- The relative weight of non-profit taxes in the effective tax burden depends on the pre-tax return.
- The ultimate value of the depreciation allowance (i.e. the amount of the interest gain) depends on the cash flows during each period. If, for example, the total amount of depreciation in one period exceeds the cash flow (and the other pre-tax earnings) in the same period there is no full tax saving due to depreciation. If there is no possibility of a loss carry back, the tax saving instead becomes effective in subsequent periods through the mechanism of a loss carry forward.

In order to find out whether the estimates for the EATR made so far are robust in terms of the assumptions made for the pre-tax return or not, the EATRs are recalculated by gradually increasing or decreasing the value for the pre-tax return in sequences of 5% compared with the base case data.

The curves in Figure 3 show that the EATR decreases with the value for the pre-tax return in all countries. The reason is that the impact of non-profit taxes and of comparatively disadvantageous depreciation allowances on the EATR become less important. In the countries that levy high real estate taxes (Ireland and the UK) or additional non-profit taxes on corporations (France and the USA), the reduction of the EATR is most evident. By contrast, it is obvious that the EATRs, in particular in France, and also in the USA rise as the pre-tax returns fall, because non-profit taxes then constitute a relatively high fraction of a smaller pre-tax return.

The results also reveal that, on the one hand, France and Germany and on the other hand the Netherlands and the UK can change their positions in the country ranking depending on the value of the pre-tax return. Both Germany and the UK can improve their position towards France and the Netherlands respectively with an increasing pre-tax return. Therefore it cannot be concluded that the French or the Dutch EATRs are always higher than the EATR in Germany and the UK respectively.

Figure 3: Effective average tax rate across 5 EU Member States and the USA
- Variation of pre tax return
- Only corporate taxes

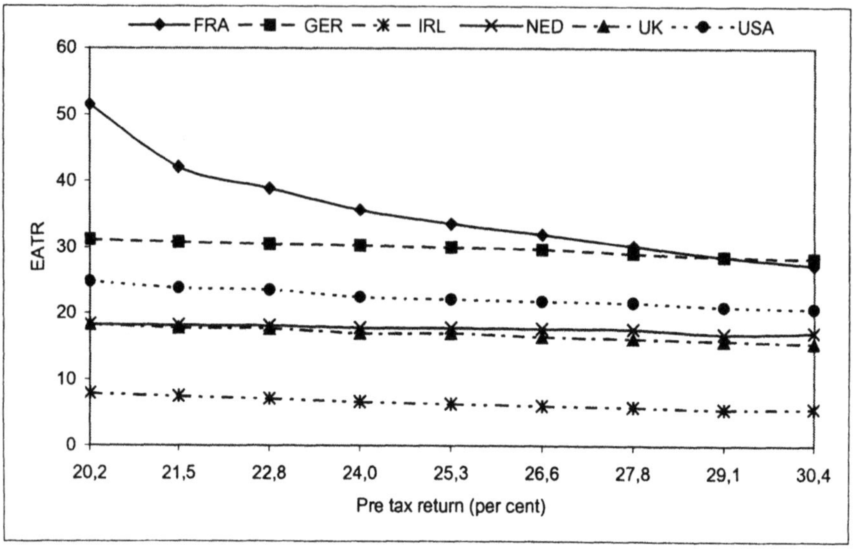

To sum up, the value of the EATR in one country as well as the differences between the national EATRs are highly sensitive to the assumption made for the value of the pre-tax return.

3.2.4 Different industries

The effective tax burden always depends on individual cases which provide the economic data for the calculation. The results of the base case scenario and the above sensitivity analysis made clear that various values exist for the EATR in one country. Therefore is it impossible to make universally valid statements regarding the differences in the EATR across countries. The EATR depends, for example, on the types of assets (investment), the sources of finance and the profitability of a company. Since the character of these factors influences the tax burden, the resultant EATR will differ from country to country.

In order to investigate the impact of alternative weights for assets, sources of finance etc., this section calculates and compares the EATR of 10 industries in addition to the base case, which referred to data from the manufacturing sector. Figure 4 shows the effective average tax burdens for corporations from the different industries as computed by the European Tax Analyzer. With respect to industries other than the manufacturing sector in Ireland, it has to be pointed out that the standard 28% corporation tax rate applies instead of the manufacturing relief of 10%. The comparison of the tax burden is based on company data regarded as typical for the selected industries.[27] In Figure 4, the average EATR of the EU-5 represents the zero line for each industry.

In Germany, there is a comparably high level of profit taxes, but only negligible non-profit taxes. From the point of view of German company, this means that the lower the profitability, the greater the tax advantage compared to other countries and vice versa. This becomes very clear if we look at the relative position of a company from the *Building and Construction* sector. In contrast to the base case manufacturing company this company has a very low level of profitability. Thus, since the EATR of this company is influenced above all by non-profit taxes, Germany's relative position in the country ranking improves. By contrast, the relative position of France deteriorates when the profitability of a company is low. This can be attributed to the high level of non-profit taxes in France.

Low profitability in comparison to the base case manufacturing company is also decisive for the more favourable German and the less favourable French position in the *Metal Production*, *Food and Beverages*, *Commerce*, and *Automotive Vehicles* sectors.

Figure 4: Effective average tax rate across 5 EU Member States and the USA
- Different industries
- Differences with reference to the average EATR of the 5 EU Member States
- Only corporate taxes

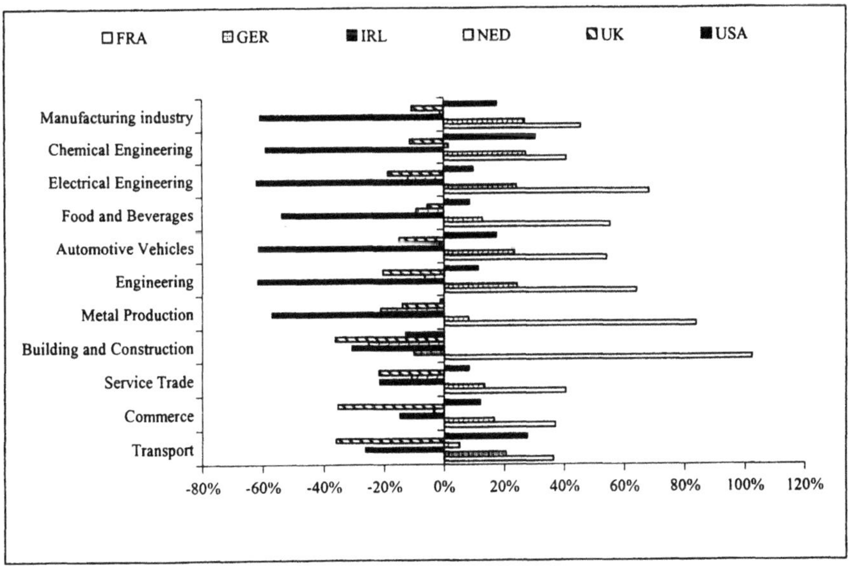

27 The data was taken from official German statistics. See Deutsche Bundesbank (1997c). The financial ratios of these industries are presented in Appendix A.

Although profitability in the *Engineering* and *Electrical Engineering* sectors is also low in comparison to the base case manufacturing company, the relative position of Germany vis a vis the UK, the Netherlands and the USA is not maintained. The reason is that in both sectors the advantages of the low profitability are overcompensated for by the effects of low capital intensity. Thus, the impact of the comparably favourable German depreciation regulations on the EATR is only minor. The reason for the improvement of Germany in comparison with France is the high personnel intensity of both industries. Since personnel expenses enter the tax bases of the "taxe professionnelle" and the employer taxes, the burden with non-profit taxes in France increases.

The *Transport industry* has favourable tax conditions in Germany. The reasons are the comparably high capital intensity and the comparably low debt-to-equity ratio. By contrast, the relative positions of the Netherlands and the USA are deteriorating.

Compared to the base case, the relative positions for the Chemical Engineering and Service Trade sectors are worse in Germany. The reason, in the case of *Chemical Engineering*, is the high equity ratio, where the discrimination against equity financing in Germany due to the trade tax on income is noticeable. In the case of the *Service Trade* sector, it is the high profitability that causes the deterioration of the German position.

The comparison reveals that different corporate economic data can effect variations in the tax burden differences between countries. With reference to Ireland, the industry as a whole has an impact on the tax burden since the 10% relief is only available for the manufacturing sector which we consider as our base case. Therefore, the relative ranking for Irish companies is worse compared to the base case. In most cases it is now the UK which takes the first place in the country ranking. On average however, Ireland is still in second place. Since the UK tax rate (30%) is higher than the Irish tax rate (28%) this indicates advantages with respect to the tax base in the UK (see also Table 10 above).

However, except for the Irish case, the industry comparison also arrives at (almost) the same ranking of countries. According to this ranking, the French tax burden is always highest followed by Germany. Except for two industries (Transport and Chemical Engineering) the tax burden in the United States is lower than in Germany. The differences between these two countries are only minor, however. Conversely, the low level of taxation in the UK, in Ireland and the Netherlands is not achieved by either France, Germany or the USA in any of the cases examined.

Compared to the EU-5 average, the average EATR of each country over the 11 selected industries, including the base case manufacturing sector, reveals the following differences: differences: France (+57.1%), Germany (+17.1%), USA (+11.8%), Netherlands (-7.6%), UK (-20.4%) and Ireland (-46.1%). Since this country ranking corresponds to the one in the base case, the base case seems to give a reliable indication of the relative position of each country.

3.3 Overall level (corporation and domestic shareholders)

Just as at the corporation level, the tax burden at the overall level (i.e. including personal taxes) is influenced by assumptions about the economic data. Of the variables that have a large impact on the overall EATR, we consider the distribution policy of the company and the sources of company finance provided by the shareholders to be the most relevant.

3.3.1 Dividend policy

In order to work out the impact of changing distribution policy assumptions on the overall EATR, the corporation's distribution rate was gradually increased from zero (i.e. full retention of profits) to 100% (i.e. full distribution of profits). The assumptions about the number and the tax status of the shareholders are the same as in the base case (i.e. 10 non tax-exempt individual domestic shareholders). Figure 5 shows the results.[28]

If the *profits are fully retained* in the corporation the overall EATR above all is influenced by the taxes of the corporation. Due to the differences between the tax burden of the corporations already explained above, the overall EATR is highest in France and lowest in Ireland.

In the case of *profit distribution*, however, the overall EATR increases with the rate of distribution in all countries. From the results, it is obvious that Germany improves its relative position in the country ranking while the positions of France, Ireland and the USA are deteriorate. Ireland and the USA even lose one place in the country ranking. This result can be attributed to a great extent to the different corporation tax systems and the progression of the income tax rates.[29]

---

28 The assumption here that the corporation basically has only domestic sources of income excludes cross-border economic activities. For an analysis of cross-border EATR using the European Tax Analyzer model see Jacobs and Spengel (1997).

29 It has to be noted that there are additional reasons based on disparities in taxation that explain the differences between the national EATR (but not the increasing EATR in the case of profit distribution). First, there are company taxes that can never be credited against personal income tax (e.g. real property tax in all countries, trade or franchise taxes on income in Germany and the USA, and non-profit taxes in France and the USA). Moreover, there are property taxes (e.g. personal net wealth taxes in France, the Netherlands, and the USA) at the level of the shareholders.

Figure 5: Effective average tax rate across 5 EU Member States and the USA
- Variation of rate of distribution
- Corporate and personal taxes

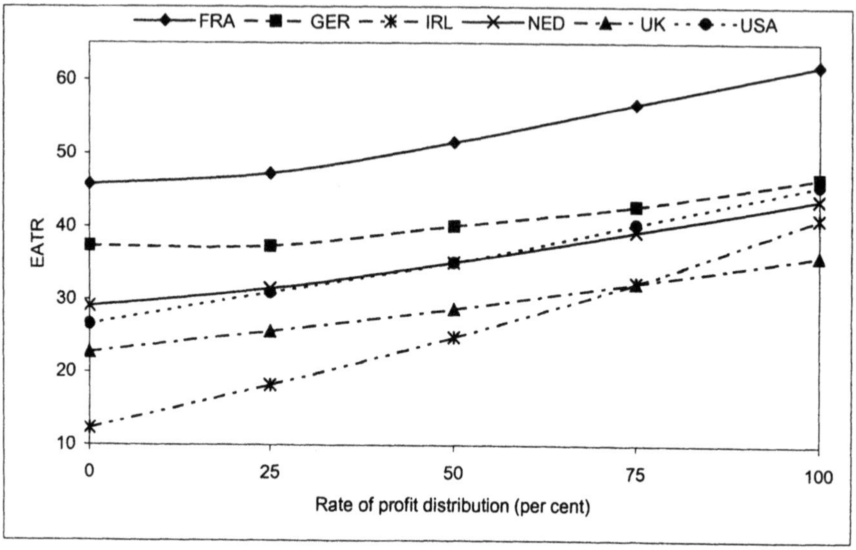

Corporation tax systems: Due to the full imputation system in Germany, the underlying corporation tax on distributed profits is merely replaced by the personal income tax of the shareholders. However, in our example, since the (average) income tax rate for a small number of shareholders is higher than the corporation tax rate, the overall EATR increases with the rate of distribution. In the other five countries the corporation tax systems do not avoid the double taxation of dividends with corporation tax and personal income tax. Either part of the underlying corporation tax (e.g. the partial imputation system in France and the shareholder relief systems in the UK and the Netherlands) or the total amount of corporation tax (e.g. classical system in Ireland and the USA) becomes a definite burden.

- *Progression of income tax rates*: From the point of view of Germany however, the advantages resulting from the full imputation system are outweighed by lower (average) income tax rates in the UK, the Netherlands, and the USA. This explains why, although they do converge towards the German rate, the British, the Irish and the Dutch overall EATRs are always lower. However, the EATR in Germany and the USA are almost equal in the case of a full distribution of profits. Only France, due to the levy of several surcharges, has a higher (average) income tax rate compared to Germany. This is an additional disadvantage in the case of profit distribution in France.

To sum up, the EATR at the overall level and the differences between the countries in an international comparison depend on the assumptions about the corporation's dividend policy. All of the countries considered in this study favour profit retention compared with profit distribution. Moreover, depending on the rate of distribution, the EATR of some countries intersects (e.g. the US EATR with the Dutch and the German). For these reasons it is impossible to make universally valid statements about the EATR at the overall level.[30]

It is interesting to note, however, that the EATRs converge with an increasing rate of distribution. The lower degree of divergence is also reflected in the range between the highest and the lowest EATR: the gap is 33.5 percentage points in the case of full retention and 25.9 percentage points in the case of full distribution.[31] Therefore, the competitive situation for small and medium-sized corporations with regard to taxation in the countries covered by this report is quite similar if the inclusion of personal taxes and a high distribution ratio are considered as relevant. The combination of different levels of corporate and personal taxes and the interaction of these taxes with the different corporation tax systems thus reduces the dispersion of the EATR at the level of the shareholders to a great extent. However, no clear pattern exists as to whether countries with high (low) EATRs at the corporate level have relatively lower (higher) EATRs at the overall level. Whereas the positions of Ireland (with a relatively low EATR at the corporate level) and France (with a relatively high EATR at the corporate level) deteriorate, Germany (with a relatively high EATR at the corporate level) and the UK (with a relatively low EATR at the corporate level) improve their positions.

3.3.2 Equity to total capital ratio

The corporation tax systems of France, Ireland, the Netherlands, the UK and the USA do not avoid double taxation of dividends. This (mitigated) double taxation occurs because the distributed profits of a corporation are taxed with personal income tax and part of the corporation tax cannot be credited against the personal income tax. By contrast, other sources of capital income (e.g. interest) are only taxed once with personal income tax. This unequal taxation of capital income can distort, inter alia, the decision of a shareholder regarding whether to finance a corporation with equity or with debt capital.[32]

This section investigates the impact of changing assumptions about the financing of the corporation on the EATR at the shareholder level. Therefore, it is assumed that the corporation is entirely financed by its shareholders with debt or equity

---

30 Moreover, the situation in the case of a great number of shareholders earning only small amounts of dividends or tax exempt or foreign shareholders can be completely different. See Jacobs et al. (1999).

31 The corresponding standard deviations fall from 11.6 (full retention) to 8.7 (full distribution). See Table B7 of Appendix B.

32 The impact of different corporation tax systems on the financing of corporations by their shareholders is analysed by Jacobs (1989), Jacobs and Spengel (1993).

capital (i.e. the corporations do not raise any funds from third parties). In the case of debt-financing, the shareholders receive interest income for the loan granted to the corporation at a fixed rate. Whereas, in the case of equity financing, the profits are fully distributed to the shareholders. The weightings of the sources of finance are gradually changed by increasing the equity to total capital ratio from 25% to 100%. Figure 6 shows the results.

Figure 6: Effective average tax rate across 5 EU Member States and the USA
- Variation of equity to total capital ratio
- Corporate and personal taxes

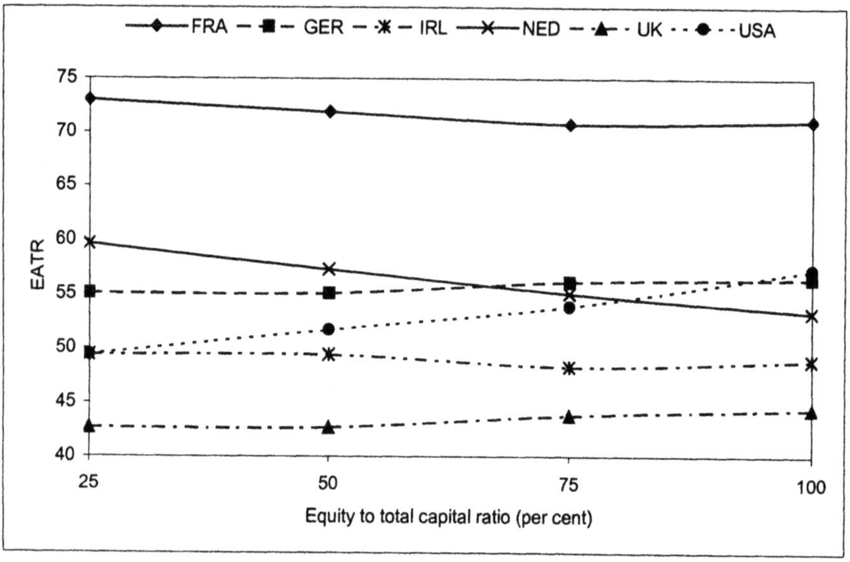

- In Germany, as can be expected from the full imputation corporation tax system, the corporation's source of finance has almost no impact on the EATR at the overall level. Therefore, a full imputation system is neutral towards financing decisions (as analysed here in a domestic context). The reason for the slight increase of the EATR with the equity to total capital ratio is the preferential treatment of debt financing within the scope of the trade tax on income (half of the interest expenses are deductible and no allowance at all is given for equity).
- As expected, EATR in the UK and the USA increase with the equity to total capital ratio. This is because the corporation tax systems in both countries (i.e. the shareholder relief system in the UK and the classical system in the USA) do not eliminate the double taxation of dividends and hence discriminate in favour of equity as opposed to debt financing.

By contrast, in Ireland, although there is a classical system, an increase of the equity ratio has almost no effect on the EATR. This significantly low disparity between equity and debt financing again – as at the corporation level – can be attributed to the low corporation tax rate. In the case of equity financing, this means that only a very small portion of the corporation tax becomes definite. As a consequence, dividends and interest payments bear an almost equal tax burden (with income and corporation tax).[33]

- Referring to the effects solely attributable to the corporation tax system, one would also expect a discrimination against equity financing in France and in the Netherlands. However, the trends of the EATR show the opposite, i.e. a discrimination against debt financing. There are of course different reasons for these results. In the Netherlands it is the combination of the corporation and personal income tax rate that results in a lower (combined) tax rate on dividends. Whereas interest income is taxed at a marginal income tax rate of 60%, dividend income is only taxed at a rate of 51.25% (i.e. corporation tax 35% plus reduced tax rate for dividends of 25% on a dividend of 65% (= 16.25%)). In France, the discrimination against equity financing caused by the partial imputation system is outweighed by a lower property tax burden on equity financing (i.e. the taxable value of shares is lower than the taxable value of loans according to the valuation rules of the French tax code).

Altogether, the results show that taxation is not entirely neutral towards the financing of a corporation in any of the countries covered by this study. Moreover, no common pattern exists as to a preferential taxation of debt or equity financing. Since there are countries that either favour debt financing (e.g. Germany and, in particular, the UK and the USA) or equity financing (e.g. France and the Netherlands) or that tax the sources of finance almost equally, both the level of the EATR and the ranking of the countries from the lowest to the highest EATR at the overall level depend on the assumptions regarding the equity to total capital ratio. In general, such dispersions are lowest in countries that either apply a full imputation system (e.g. Germany) or – irrespective of the corporation tax system – apply a low corporation tax rate (e.g. Ireland). In addition, another important prerequisite for neutrality towards company financing is an equal treatment of the dividends and interest payments with respect to income tax (and of shares and loans with respect to private property taxes).

33 Interest income is taxed at a marginal income tax rate of 46%. Dividends are taxed at a marginal rate of 51.4% (i.e. corporation tax 10% plus income tax on dividends of 46% on a dividend of 90% (= 41.4%)). However, as the taxable dividend income is reduced by the (definite) corporation tax, the average income tax rate as applied in the model is even lower.

3.4 Conclusions

A number of sensitivity analyses were carried out both with and without personal taxes. At the level of the corporation we considered alternative assumptions on the investment policy, the structure of finance and the profitability of the company as well as on the industry as a whole. In so doing, the EATRs of 10 other industries were calculated. At the shareholder level, we considered alternative assumptions regarding the distribution policy of the company and the sources of company finance provided by the shareholders.

The broad conclusions that were drawn for the base case with reference to the *corporation level* do not seem to be affected. It has to be stressed, however, that the relative position of the countries cannot be generalised. It has been shown that individual circumstances and very extreme assumptions can cause both France and Germany as well as the Netherlands and the UK to change their positions.

At the *shareholder level*, in contrast to the corporation level, there is much more variation in the EATR and the country ranking. In particular, this finding can be attributed to the different corporation tax systems, the progression of the income tax rates and the schedular treatment of different sources of capital income (i.e. the dividend and interest income of the shareholders). Therefore, it is not possible to make universally valid statements about the EATR at the overall level. One can however, draw a broad conclusion concerning the average EATR of the EU Member States. The average EATR converges (diverges) as more profits are distributed to the shareholders (retained in the corporation). Thus, differences between corporate and personal taxes and the corporation tax systems seem to be minimised in situations where most of the corporate profits are also subject to personal taxes.

Another result of the sensitivity analyses (which is confirmed by many other studies) is that the tax systems of the countries covered by this report are far from neutral. The results clearly show that taxation distorts corporations' investment and financing decisions in every country. It is important to note that, in general, the lower the statutory tax rates, the lower these distortions tend to be.

4 Effects of the German tax reform 2001

The analysis so far has been based on the tax regimes which were effective in 1999. Although there have been several changes in the tax regimes since that time, we have not incorporated any of them. However, we have taken account of the German tax reform because it seems to be an important and – with respect to the tax changes – substantial reform. Most of the tax changes will become effective as of January 1, 2001.

The principle aims of the German tax reform are to encourage investment, to strengthen international competitiveness and to restructure the tax system so that it fits with the principle goals of the Common Market in Europe. The key issues are a reduction of the (corporate and personal) income tax rates, a broadening of the base and a change in the corporation tax system.

We do not intend to give a complete overview on the tax reform here.[34] Instead, we briefly summarise the major tax changes which are of relevance for our calculations (section 4.1). Further, we describe how the EATR at the corporation level (section 4.2) and at the shareholder level (section 4.3) will be affected by the reform. The full set of tables from sections 2 and 3 including the results of the reformed German tax system is presented in Appendix B.

4.1 Description of major tax changes

Beginning on or after January 1, 2001, the German tax reform will change the corporation tax system, reduce corporation and personal income tax rates and broaden the tax base.

- *Corporation tax system*: The full imputation system that has been in force since 1977 will be abolished and instead a shareholder relief system will be introduced. Under the new system (which is similar to the system in Luxembourg), only one half of the dividends received by a private shareholder are subject to personal income tax. At the same time, all deductions connected with dividend income from the income tax base are halved. However, other elements of the private capital income such as interest receipts are still taxed at the full rate.
  The abolition of the (full) imputation system follows an international trend. After the German tax reform only five EU Member States remain which apply an imputation system: Finland, France, Italy, Portugal and Spain. The vast

34 This has been done elsewhere. See, for example, Endres and Oestreicher (2000).

majority of the Member States now utilise shareholder relief systems. The trends in the development of the tax systems is analysed in more detail in section 5.

- *Corporation tax rates*: The changes in the corporation tax rate cover both the structure and the level of the tax rate. The split-rate that distinguishes between retained (40%) and distributed profits (30%) will be abolished and a single uniform tax rate of 25% will be introduced.

  Although the 25% corporation tax rate is the second lowest of the countries considered in this report (and within the EU), the solidarity levy of 5.5% and the trade tax with an average rate of 17.56% remain. This will reduce the statutory tax rate on retained earnings from currently 52.35% to 39.3%.[35] Although this is a significant reduction, the statutory tax rate is still high compared with EU standards. Only France, at 40%, has a higher tax rate (see Table 9 above).

- *Income tax rates*: The marginal personal income tax rates will be lowered from 53% (55.92% including the solidarity levy of 5.5%) in three successive steps leading to a rate of 42% (44.31% including the solidarity levy) in 2005. The marginal tax rate begins at a taxable income of Euro 52,152. The year 2001 will set the marginal rate at 48.5% and the year 2003 at 47%. For the purposes of the following calculations we will consider only the situation up from the year 2005.

- *Corporation tax base*: There will be a broadening of the tax base by cutting back the depreciation rules both for tangible fixed assets and for buildings. The maximum declining balance rate for tangible fixed assets will be reduced from 30% to 20%. For buildings, the straight-line depreciation will be reduced from 4% to 3%.

  The impact of these tax changes on the EATR will be calculated in the following sections.

4.2 Changes of the tax burden at the level of the corporation

4.2.1 Base case scenario

As noted above, Appendix B contains a full set of tables with the results for Germany after the tax reform. This section only highlights the major impacts of

---

35 These rates include solidarity levy of 5.5% and assume an average trade tax of 17.56% which is deductible from the corporation tax base (39.3% = 17.56% + ((100-17.56)*25% = 20.61%) + 20.61 * 5.5% = 1.13%).

the German tax reform on the EATR at the level of the corporation. Table 12 compares the tax burdens for the base case corporation of the manufacturing sector in 1999 and after the tax reform (denoted as 2001).[36] The pre-tax reform results were taken from Table 4. Moreover, Table 13 lists in detail the EATR decreases and increases that can be attributed to the tax rule changes considered here.

Table 12: Effective average tax rate in Germany before and after the reform - Only corporate taxes

	GER 1999	GER 2001	Difference in %
EATR corporation			
- effective in Euro	11,290,464	10,503,163	-6.9
- effective in %	32.8	30.1	-8.2
Corporation tax incl. surcharges	8,689,994	6,891,882	-20.7
Trade tax	2,517,630	3,504,603	39.2
Real property tax	82,840	106,678	28.8

The tax reform reduces the EATR of the typical German corporation from the manufacturing sector over the calculation period of 10 years by 8.2%. The analysis of the impact of the different measures reveals that the decrease of the effective tax burden that can be attributed to the reduction of the corporation tax rate is outweighed by more than 50% by the changes in the depreciation rules and the corporation tax system (see Table 13). The reduction of the effective tax burden which is solely attributable to the lower corporation tax rate is 23.4%. The new depreciation rules for buildings and tangible fixed assets increase the average tax base[37] by 7.1% and the effective tax burden by 5.5% (buildings 1.3% and tangible fixed assets 4.2%). The EATR increase due to the change in the corporation tax system is 11%. This requires some explanation. It is assumed here that the amount of dividends distributed to the shareholders after the reform is the same as before the reform. Since the dividends are no longer accompanied by a tax credit, the corporation must increase its cash distribution in order to pay the same amount of dividends to the shareholders as before the reform.

36 At the corporation level, the EATR does not change during the period 1999-2000. See section 5 for details.

37 Except for production costs, the elements of the tax base do not change.

Table 13: Effective average tax rate in Germany before and after the reform
- Increases and Decreases attributed to different changes in taxation
- Only corporate taxes

EATR at the level of the corporation in 1999 in Euro (Table 12)		11,290,464	in % of 1999 EATR
Reduction of corporation tax rate to 25%	-	2,645,450	-23.4
Reduction of straight-line depreciation for buildings	+	143,034	1.3
Reduction of declining balance depreciation	+	473,738	4.2
Abolition of full imputation system	+	1,241,377	11.0
EATR at the level of the corporation in 2001 in Euro (Table 12)	=	10,503,163	93.1

Finally, referring to the weight of the different taxes in the EATR, the results from Table 12 show that a decrease in the corporation tax (-20.7%) is accompanied by an increase of both the trade tax (39.2%) and the real property tax (28.8%). Since both local taxes are deductible as business expenses from the base of the corporation tax, and the corporation tax rate is reduced, the (corporation) tax savings due to the deduction of these taxes will also be lower. Moreover, the change in the depreciation rules immediately affects the trade tax since it is based on the same taxable profits as the corporation tax.

Altogether, the EATR reduction is too low to improve the relative position of Germany in the country ranking. Before the reform, the German corporations' EATR (32.8%) was second highest after France (39.7%). After the reform, Germany is still second highest (30.1%) now closely followed by the USA (29.7%). There is still a considerable gap to the Netherlands (24%) in fourth position. Moreover, according to the latest reform proposals, it is likely that France is going to improve its position in the future (see section 5 for an outlook).

4.2.2 Different industries

With respect to the changes of the depreciation rules and the corporation tax system, it seems likely that the German tax reform will have a different impact on companies from different industries. Therefore, the effects on the base case company's EATR cannot be generalised. Instead, they depend on the individual structure of a company. If we consider again companies with economic data which is typical for the 10 additional industries it is evident that not all companies benefit from the reform. There is a range from a reduction in the EATR of 11% (Metal Production) to an increase of the EATR of 10.5% (Transport). Altogether, four industries suffer from a higher effective tax burden (Chemical Engineering, Automotive Vehicles, Building & Construction and Transport). In order to analyse the effects of the tax reform in more detail we distinguish between the effects of the reduction of the corporation tax rate, the broadening of the corporation tax base and the abolition of the full imputation system. Table 14 shows the impact of each measure for 10 industries[38] in detail and Figure 7 highlights the overall effects.

Table 14: Effective average tax rate in Germany before and after the reform
- Increases and Decreases attributed to different changes in taxation
- Different industries
- Only corporate taxes

	Overall decrease (-) or increase (+) of EATR (%)	Decrease of EATR (%) due to reduction of corporation tax rate to 25%	Increase of EATR (%) due to reduction of depreciation rates	Increase of EATR (%) due to abolition of full imputation system
Manufacturing industry (Base case)	-6.9	-23.4	+5.5	+11.0
Chemical Engineering	+1.5	-24.6	+6.1	+20.0
Electrical Engineering	-5.5	-23.3	+5.5	+12.3
Food & Beverages	-3.3	-20.6	+10.0	+7.3
Automotive Vehicles	+5.1	-21.7	+8.3	+18.5
Engineering	-5.9	-22.3	+5.0	+11.4
Metal Production	-11.0	-22.2	+7.7	+3.5
Building & Construction	+2.1	-18.3	+8.8	+11.6
Service Trade	-1.1	-20.4	+2.2	+17.1
Commerce	-4.5	-20.2	+4.3	+11.4
Transport	+10.5	-19.2	+18.9	+10.8

Ultimately, the effects stem from the individual company data. In this respect, the capital intensity and the distribution ratio are highly relvant. All companies benefit from the *reduction in the corporation tax rate to 25%* to almost the same degree. The reductions in the effective tax burdens vary between 18.3% (Building & Construction) and 24.9% (Chemical Engineering). The reason for the similarity is that none of the companies is currently in a loss situation. Therefore, a reduction of the tax rate is effective immediately.

In particular, Transport and Food & Beverages suffer from the *broader tax base* (i.e. reduction in depreciation allowances on buildings and tangible fixed assets). This result originates from their relatively high capital intensity of 54.1% (Transport) and 36.6% (Food & Beverages) respectively. In the Transport Industry, the extra burden almost offsets the benefit from the reduction of the tax

38 See Appendix A for the companies' financial ratios.

rate. By contrast, since both industries have a relatively low capital intensity, Service Trade and Commerce barely suffer from the reduction in depreciation allowances.

Finally, the *abolition of the full imputation system* has some effects. If we assume that the amount of dividends which is distributed to the shareholders is the same after the reform, there is a considerable increase in the effective tax burden. Since there is no tax credit available in the new system, the cash dividend must rise accordingly. The increases of the effective tax burdens vary between 3.5% (Metal Production) and 20% (Chemical Engineering). This particular result is strongly connected to the distribution ratio which is 11.3% for Metal Production and 51.9% for Chemical Engineering.

Figure 7: Change in effective average tax rate in Germany before and after the reform
- Different industries
- Only corporate taxes

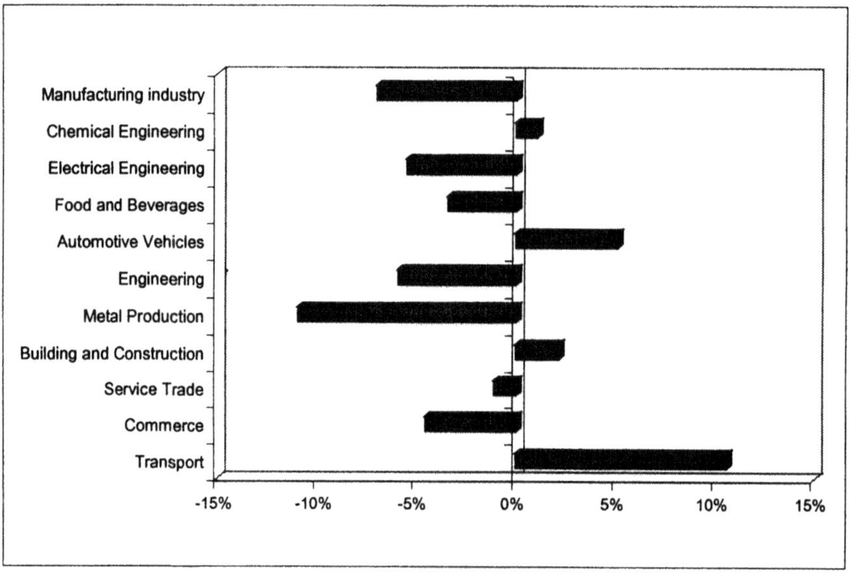

All in all, companies with capital intensive production and high distribution ratios suffer most from the German tax reform. By contrast, companies with personnel intensive production and which retain most of their profits benefit from the reform. It has been shown that the impact of the German tax reform depends to a great extent on the assumptions regarding the distribution ratio. Consequently, the relative position of Germany in the country ranking can be higher or lower compared to the base case. There is, however, no industry that wins or looses more than one position in the ranking. Therefore, the broad conclusions for the base case company of the manufacturing sector are not affected.

4.3 Changes of the tax burden at the overall level (corporation and domestic shareholders)

If we consider the overall level including personal taxes of the shareholders, the German tax reform reduces the effective tax burden significantly. If we look ahead to the situation in the year 2005, when the marginal income tax rate will be 42% (instead of 53% in 1999), the effective burden with personal taxes is reduced by 37.1% (see Table 15). In addition to the reduction of the marginal (and average) income tax rate, which affects both the dividend and interest income, this result can be attributed to the introduction of the new corporation tax system. According to the German method of shareholder relief (which is similar to the one in Luxembourg) only one half of the dividends are subject to personal income tax. The results in Table 15 which combine corporate and personal taxes show that the overall EATR will fall from 37.4% in 1999 to 30.1% in 2005.[39] As a result Germany advances by two positions in the country ranking to the third lowest place behind Ireland (17.2%) and the UK (25.6%).

Table 15: Effective average tax rate in Germany before and after the reform - Corporate and personal taxes

	GER 1999	GER 2001 / 2005	Difference in %
EATR corporation			
- effective in Euro	11,290,464	10,503,163	-6.9
- effective in %	32.8	30.1	-8.2
EATR shareholder			
Income tax	4,249,136	2,674,425	-37.1
EATR overall level			
- effective in Euro	15,539,600	13,177,588	-15.2
- effective in %	37.4	30.1	-19.5

A full set of tables from sections 2 and 3 which include the results of the reformed German tax system is presented in Appendix B. The results of combining the sensitivity analysis carried out in section 3 with the new German tax regime show that after the reform the EATR at the overall level, irrespective of the assumptions on the dividend policy and the financing policy of the corporation, will be lower. This implies that the tax reform is always beneficial at the overall level. In

39 The German EATR at the overall level would be 31.0% for the year 2001.

particular, in contrast to the situation at the corporation level, there seems to be no disadvantage resulting from the change of the corporation tax system.

Figure 8: Effective average tax rate in Germany before and after the reform
- Variation of distribution rate
- High and low (= base case) number of shareholders
- Corporate and personal taxes

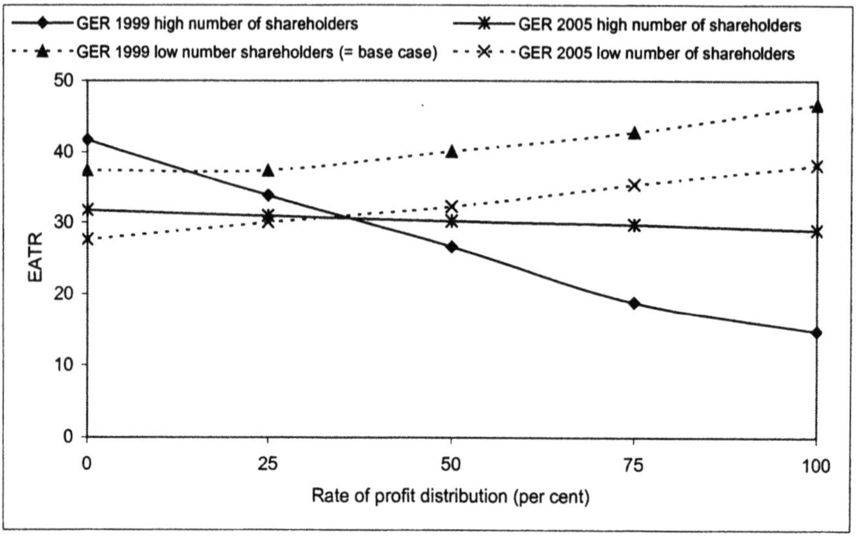

Nevertheless, one has to bear in mind that the calculations in our base case are based on the assumption that the company is medium-sized with a low number of shareholders. This in turn means that the average income tax rate will always be relatively high. If we instead consider a corporation which has such a high number of shareholders that the dividend income can be collected by each shareholder without paying taxes thereon,[40] the result is different. Figure 8 shows the EATR at the overall level if the rate of distribution of the corporation was gradually increased from zero (i.e. full retention of profits) to 100% (i.e. full distribution of profits). In contrast to the base with 10 shareholders shown in Figure 5 above, this sensitivity analysis also considers a case with a high number of shareholders, each paying no personal taxes on dividend income.[41]

In the former full imputation system, the EATR for a high number of shareholders tends to fall constantly with an increase of the distribution rate. The minimum value (of 14.8% in our example) corresponds to the definite burden with the trade tax. In the new shareholder relief system, there is only a small variation in the

---

40 In Germany, besides the general allowance of Euro 7,664, there is an allowance for capital income of Euro 1,534.

41 Sometimes this is known as a situation with "zero-rated shareholders".

EATR, which is consistently around 30%. The reason is that, previously, in the imputation system distributed profits were always only subject to personal income tax. If the nominal personal income tax on the grossed-up dividend income (i.e. including the corporation tax credit) was lower than the underlying corporation tax, the amount of excess corporation tax was refunded to the shareholder. In extreme cases only a definite burden with trade tax, which was never credited against personal income tax or refunded, remained. By contrast, in the new shareholder relief system, the corporation tax, in addition to the trade tax, also always becomes definite.[42]

As a result, for the overall level, it seems reasonable to conclude that a typical medium-sized corporation with a low number of shareholders benefits from the German tax reform. By contrast, the EATR is likely to rise for a company with a high number of low tax shareholders. This may be a more likely situation for multinational companies. Nonetheless, it is not clear whether this unequal tax treatment of shareholders will have any impact on the investment pattern of companies since only the ability of the shareholders with respect to their savings is affected by the tax reform.

4.4 Conclusions

The German tax reform which will take effect in 2001 is an important tax reform within the EU. It replaces the full imputation tax system with a split rate and introduces a shareholder relief system with a single rate structure, it reduces the corporate and personal income tax rates and finally, it broadens the tax base. Despite these changes and the considerable reduction of the EATR at the *level of the corporation*, the German tax reform has only minor effects on the relative position of Germany in the country ranking. Although the EATR falls by 8.2%, the base case medium-sized corporation in the manufacturing sector cannot improve its position in the country ranking from the lowest to the highest EATR. The reason could be the statutory tax rate on profits, which at 39.3%, is still second highest in comparison with the other countries.

From the results of the sensitivity analyses including 10 other selected industries, one may conclude that there could be some impact on investment and financing patterns of corporations. It has been shown that companies with capital intensive production and high distribution ratios will suffer from the results of the German tax reform. By contrast, companies with personnel intensive production and a high

42 This conclusion, however, is only valid for the case of a company with a considerable number of domestic shareholders. If a multinational corporation with a considerable number of non-resident shareholders is considered instead, the change of the corporation tax system has almost no effect. The reason is that non-resident shareholders were never entitled to a tax credit.

ratio of retained profits will benefit. However, even with respect to the additional 10 companies, the changes in Germany's country ranking are only minor.

Finally, with reference to the taxation of the shareholders, there is a significant reduction in the EATR only if one takes a medium-sized company as typical. By contrast, since there is no entitlement for (the refund of) a corporation tax credit anymore, the EATR at the overall level is likely to rise for a (multinational) company with a high number of domestic shareholders.

5 Changes of the effective average tax burden since 1995

This section summarises the main tax reforms and their consequences for the EATR both for the corporations level and that of the shareholders. The aspects of the tax systems referred to and entered in the calculations of the EATR are those that apply to the manufacturing sector and that are generally available. This excludes, as it does for all sectors considered in this report, above all, special investment incentive schemes.

In our analysis we refer to the period 1995-2001 and incorporate the effects of the German tax reform for the whole period. As far as personal taxes are concerned, the calculations for Germany already take the tax rate reductions for the year 2005 into account. Furthermore, we include the tax reform proposal in France (see Jouanjan, 2000, Lefebvre, 2000) that has been announced for the near future (we denote this situation also as the year 2001). Therefore, the results for the period 2001 also present an outlook on the future development of the tax systems. The results of the calculations are also presented in Appendix C.

5.1 Changes of the tax burden at the level of the corporation

The results for the *corporation level* in Figure 9 show that in the period 1995-1999 the EATR has declined in Germany and the UK, has risen in France and in Ireland, and has not changed in the Netherlands. As a consequence, the average EATR for the EU-5 declined from 25.5% (1995) to 25.1% (1999). With the exception of France, the EATR did not change during the period 1999-2000. The German tax reform and the announced tax reform in France will cause a further reduction of the average EATR to 22.7% (2001). At the same time there is also less dispersion sincc the standard deviation in the EU-5 decreases from 11.7 (1995) to 8.0 (2001). The EATR in the USA, which was constant during the period 1999-2001, is 29.7% and thus above EU-5 average. From the results it seems reasonable to conclude that in particular the countries with relatively high EATR – Germany and France – are tending to reduce their tax burden. In light of these findings, the situation in Germany shows a clear trend beginning in 1997.

The dominant trend in the tax reforms has been the *lowering of the statutory tax rates on profits*. This has been seen in three out of five EU Member States:

France: The basic statutory corporation tax rate is 33.33%. However, there are several surcharges on the corporation tax. The tax reform in 2000 reduced the rate of the corporate surtax from 20% to 10% and introduced a new surcharge of 3.3%

(contribution sociale sur les bénéfices des sociétés). Therefore, the statutory corporation tax rate was reduced from 40% to 37.77%. The proposed tax reform aims to abolish these surcharges until the year 2003. From that point on the basic statutory corporation tax rate of 33.33% would be in force again.

- *Germany*:[43] The statutory corporation tax rate on retained earnings was reduced form 45% to 40% (1999). The solidarity levy on corporation and personal income tax has fallen from 7.5% to 5.5% (1998). The tax reform becoming effective from January 1, 2001, introduces a uniform corporation tax rate for retained and distributed profits of 25%. If the trade tax and solidarity levy are added, this results in a statutory tax rate on profits of 39.3% (compared to 52.35% in the year 2000).
- *United Kingdom*: The statutory corporation tax rate has fallen from 33% to 31% (1998) and then to 30% (1999).[44]

Figure 9: Effective average tax rate across 5 EU Member States and the USA
- Period 1995-2001
- Only corporate taxes

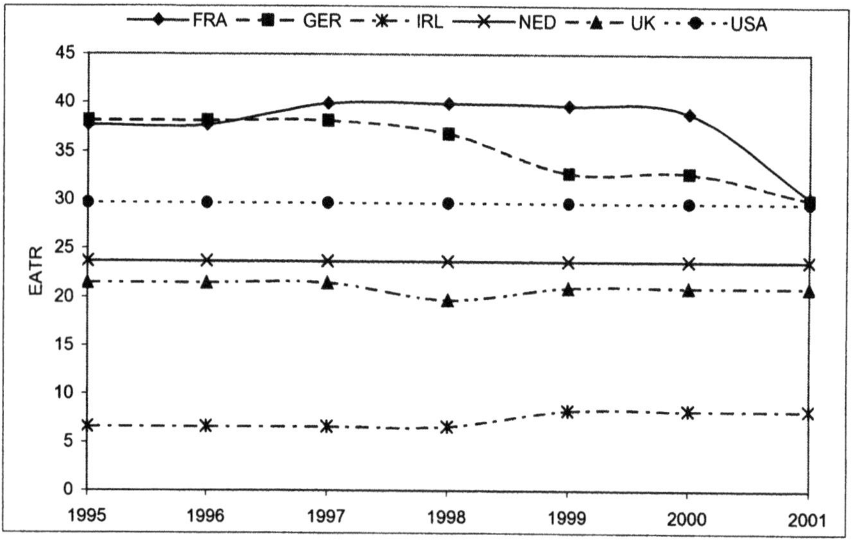

---

43 The fact that the average tax rate (Hebesatz) of the trade tax on income levied by German municipalities has risen over the period 1995-2000 must also be considered. Therefore, the calculated decline of the EATR is less than expected solely from the reduction of the corporation tax rate.

44 However, the tax rate reduction in 1999 did not effect an increase in the EATR at the corporation level because the imputation system was abolished at the same time (see below).

As in earlier periods not covered by this study, the lowering of the tax rates was combined with extensions of the *tax base*.[45] An exception has to be made for the UK which reduced tax rates without broadening the tax base. Nevertheless, the tax rate reductions in the UK were only minor. By contrast, in Germany, the tax rate reductions in 1999 were largely financed by cutting back tax incentives, a long list of completely disallowing the deduction of certain expenses, and changes in tax accounting that led to a deferral of the tax deductibility of many expenditures until closer to the time it is actually incurred (see Endres and Ditsch, 1999: 89-99, for an overview and comments). The tax reform in the year 2001 introduced a further broadening of the tax base by cutting back the depreciation rules both for machinery (declining balance only 20 instead of 30%) and buildings (straight-line depreciation over 33 instead of 25 years). These extensions of the tax base have been considered in the above calculations. In France, the government intends to decrease the coefficients of the declining balance depreciation method by 0.25% in order to compensate for the revenue loss due to the tax rate reductions.

However, the lowering of the tax rate has not been the only type of reform. During the period 1995-1998 France raised the statutory corporation tax rate by surcharges of 10% (1995) and 15% (1997) from 33.33% to 41.67%. Finally, as already pointed out above, the surcharges totalling 25% were reduced to their current level of 13.33%.

Two trends, that are important for the competitive effects of taxation with reference to the *structure of the national tax systems*, have to emphasised:

- *Non-profit taxes*: Germany has abolished property taxes (1997) and the trade tax on capital (1998). In 1999 France gradually started to exempt payrolls from the base of the „taxe professionnelle" by granting special deductions. Moreover, a 100% exemption until the year 2003 for payrolls has been announced. This has already been incorporated in the above calculations for the year 2001.

Corporation tax systems: Since 1997, the Netherlands has applied a shareholder relief system for qualified shareholders (participation of at least 5%)[46] instead of the classical system that is still in force for non-qualified shareholders. The Dutch shareholder relief provides a reduced income tax rate on dividends of 25% instead of 60% as on other items of income. Great Britain abolished its imputation system in 1999 and also introduced a kind of shareholder relief system. Companies no longer have to pay the so-called advance corporation tax (ACT) which was equal to the tax credit of 20%. As of 1999, the tax credit has been reduced to 10%

---

45 For an overview of the tax reforms in earlier years see, for example, Chennells and Griffith (1997: 26-30), Rimbaux (1996: 92-127). Both studies, however, omit non-profit taxes.

46 Since our model firm in the base case considers ten shareholders with identical participation (i.e. 10%), the shareholder relief applies.

regardless of the corporation tax paid by the company. At the same time, a special upper income tax rate on dividends of 32.5% (instead of 40% for ordinary income) was introduced. This reduction, together with the reduced tax credit ensures, however, that individual shareholders are facing the same post-tax dividend income as before the tax reform (see Gammie 1998: 434-435 for details). Ireland also abolished the partial imputation system by gradually reducing the tax credit (ACT) from 23/77 (1995) to 21/79 (1997) and 11/89 (1998). Finally, the tax credit was abolished in 1999. This means that Ireland has applied a classical system since 1999. Although the system involving entering the 10% manufacturing relief in the above calculations was not affected by the gradual reduction of the ACT, the classical system has nevertheless applied since 1999. Germany has abolished the full imputation system and introduced a shareholder relief in its tax reform for the year 2001. The shareholder relief provides that 50% of the dividends received are exempt from personal income tax. The new German system is described in greater detail in section 4 above.

5.2 Changes of the tax burden at the overall level (corporation and domestic shareholders)

The trend of the EATR at the *shareholder level* shown in Figure 10 closely follows the trend at the corporation level: For the period 1995-1999 the EATR declined in three countries (Germany, the Netherlands and the UK) and risen in France and Ireland. Except for France and Ireland, the EATR did not change from 1999 to 2000. The average EATR for the EU-5 declined from 34.0% (1995) to 32.2% (1999) and 31.9% (2000) respectively. A further reduction to 28.9% (2001) can be attributed to the tax reforms in Germany and France. In contrast to the corporation level , the EATR in the USA (which remained at 32.0% over the whole period) ranges below EU-5 average except for the last two periods.

In most cases, the development of the EATR at the overall level can be attributed to the tax changes at the corporate level which have already been discussed above. In addition to the important effects due to the changes in the corporation tax systems, only minor effects remain that solely affect the taxation of shareholders. For example, in France there are various surcharges on private investment income (including interest and dividend income) which have been increased from 4.9% to 10% during the period 1995-1997. Finally, capital taxes at the corporation level, were gradually removed. In addition to corporate property tax, Germany abolished property tax for individuals (1997). The Netherlands also reduced their property tax rate for individuals (1998).

Figure 10: Effective average tax rate across 5 EU Member States and the USA
- Period 1995-2001
- Corporate and personal taxes

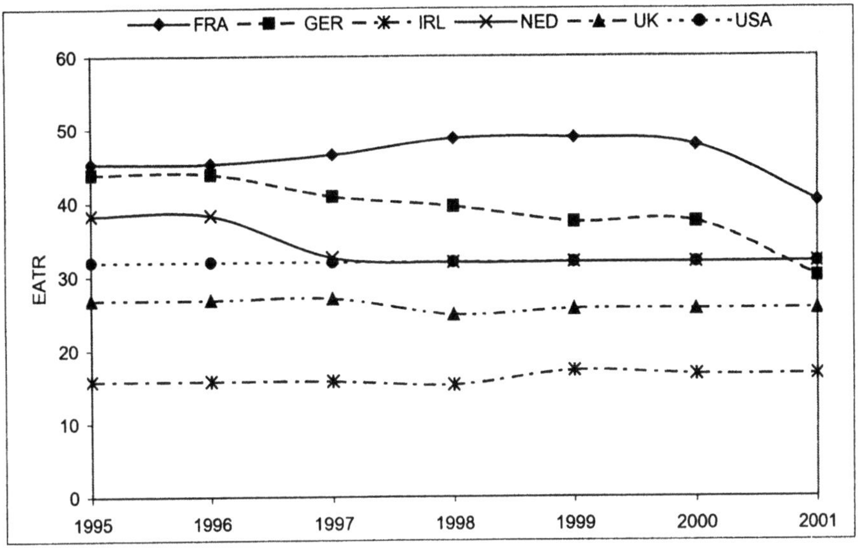

5.3 Conclusions

The development of effective tax burdens since 1995, including reform proposals for the year 2001 and subsequent periods, can be summarised as follows. In particular those countries covered by this study which had or still have a relatively high EATR are demonstrating a tendency towards a significant reduction in their effective tax burdens (e.g. Germany and France). Germany, for example, could improve its position in the country ranking by one (corporation level) or two places (overall level). On the other hand, there are only minor reductions in the burdens of those countries where the EATR is already relatively low (e.g. Ireland).

The dominant trend in the decrease of the EATR has been a reduction in the statutory tax rates on profits. However, tax rate reductions were not the only reason for the decrease of the EATR. From a systematic point of view, the gradual abolition of non-profit taxes (Germany, France and Netherlands) and the trend towards an implementation of shareholder relief corporation tax systems or a trend against imputation systems have to be emphasised. Germany, Ireland and the UK have all abolished their imputation systems. Of these countries, Germany and the UK have introduced shareholder relief systems and Ireland has established the classical system. A shareholder relief system was also introduced in the Netherlands, but only for qualified shareholders.

As a result of the reforms the average EATR have converged both at the corporation level and the overall level. Since countries with relatively low EATRs did not reduce their tax burden remarkably, however, there is no so-called race to the bottom. In spite of the gradual convergence of the EATR one cannot conclude, that tax distortions due to competition were reduced significantly or disappeared. Instead, the differences between the EATR are still high. As the results of the sensitivity analysis in section 3 show, there still can be a considerable variation in the EATR.

6 Impact of hypothetical tax reforms in the EU

6.1 Overview on simulations

This section considers the impact of hypothetical tax reforms on the effective tax burdens which were calculated and analysed in the previous sections. Since there is no initiative in this respect, the scenarios for tax reforms should not be regarded as proposals for reforming or harmonising company taxation in Europe. The results from these scenarios should rather help to identify and analyse the impact of different elements of the tax regimes on the effective tax burden. It is important both for policy makers and investors to have an idea about the weight of the different tax drivers in the effective average tax burden (EATR), i.e. to identify the relative weight of the tax bases, the tax rates, the different types of taxes and the corporation tax system in the EATR separately. Therefore, the scenarios for tax reforms are divided into three categories: elements of the corporation tax base, the corporation tax rate including local taxes and the corporation tax system.

National policy makers might want to know, for example, which element of their tax regime is most important for attracting foreign investors. *Multinational policy makers* might be interested to know the elements of different tax regimes which are most decisive for variations of EATR between countries. Finally, with respect to the ongoing discussion regarding unfair tax competition (see European Commission, 2000, OECD, 1998, OECD, 2000b), knowledge of the tax drivers' respective weightings in the EATR helps both *national and multinational policy makers* identify harmful tax measures. For example, this information could be helpful in deciding, with respect to the level of the effective tax burden, whether generous elements of the tax base (e.g. certain book reserves in the balance sheet) are more harmful than a generous (reduced) tax rate and vice versa. The interests of *international investors* are similar to those of policy makers. When international investors are deciding where to locate a subsidiary or where to increase investment, they cannot take into account each single element of the tax regime. With regard to location and investment decisions, the process of tax planning is very difficult.[47] Therefore it is important to know which elements of a tax regime are most decisive in determining of the effective tax burden (i.e. the tax rate, the tax base, the tax system or local taxes).

The simulations listed in Box 2 consider 15 different scenarios. For each scenario one of the three particular elements (tax base, tax rate including local taxes and tax system) of the tax regimes is harmonised across the 5 EU Member States considered here (France, Germany, Ireland, Netherlands and UK) plus – for the

---

47 For empirical evidence see Devereux (1992).

sake of comparison – the USA. By setting just one element of the different tax regimes equal across all countries, it is possible to identify the effect of this particular element on the level and also on the variation of the effective tax burdens, and hence on the possible distortion of competition within the countries under consideration. Each simulation considers only the medium-sized company in the base case using typical data for the manufacturing sector (see section 1.4 for details). Except for Germany, the scenarios are based – as in the previous sections – on the tax regimes which were effective in the fiscal year 1999. Since the German tax reform brought significant changes and the simulations are intended to give an outlook on the near future, the reformed German tax regime will be considered in this section.[48]

Box 2: Classification of simulations

A. Corporation tax base

1. Common depreciation on intangibles. Straight-line over 5 years (20%).
2. Common depreciation on buildings. Straight-line over 25 years (4%).
3. Common SL depreciation on tangible fixed assets. Straight-line over the estimated periods of economic use (5 to 10 years depending on type of asset).
4. Common DB depreciation on tangible fixed assets. Declining balance at 3 times straight-line over the estimated periods of economic use, at a maximum of 30%.
5. Common valuation of inventories. Full costs and LIFO allocation.
6. Common allocation of pension costs (book reserve German type). Allowing to build up a book reserve for pensions as in Germany.
7. Common allocation of pension costs (pension fund US type). Allowing funded schemes as in the Anglo-Saxon countries.
8. Common book reserves for bad debts. Future guarantee payments within next 2 years, 2% of annual turnover.
9. Common overall tax base (IAS). Depreciation methods according to (1)-(3) above, depreciation periods are 5 years for intangibles, 40 and 50 years for buildings, 5 to 10 years for tangible fixed assets, valuation of inventories according to (5), allocation of pension costs according to (7), no provisions for bad debts.

48 This means that the calculations on the corporate level are based on the rules for the year 2001. At the overall level which includes shareholder taxation we refer to year 2005. See section 4 for details.

Continuation Box 2:

B. Corporation tax rate and local taxes

10. Common corporation tax rate, including surcharges but excluding local taxes, at EU average of 32.28%.
11. Common corporation tax rate, including surcharges and local profit taxes, at EU average of 33.84%.
12. Common corporation tax rate of 25%, including surcharges and local profit taxes.
13. Common corporation tax rate of 25%, including surcharges and all (profit and non-profit) local taxes.

C. Corporation tax system

14. Common corporation tax system. Classical system (only corporate taxes).
15. Common corporation tax system. Classical system (corporate and personal taxes).

The following analyses concentrate mainly on the impact of the reform scenarios on the effective tax burden of corporations. However, Appendix D also provides results including personal taxes.[49] The Tables in this section present the EATR for each simulation in each country. They also present the average EATR and the standard deviations from the average EATR across the 5 EU Member States for each simulation. These statistics should help to identify the remaining variation in the effective tax burdens after each reform scenario.

[49] Moreover, for the sake of comparison, Appendix D also provides results for the former German tax regime (i.e. year 1999) and Ireland applying the regular 28% corporation tax rate.

6.2 Reforming the corporation tax bases

The 9 simulations listed in Part A of Box 2 refer to corporation tax bases. The results of each simulation are presented in Table 16. The first 8 of these simulations consider only a single element of the tax base. By contrast, since it analyses the effects of an uniform tax base in all EU Member States based on the "International Accounting Standards", simulation 9 considers several elements simultaneously. However, all other elements of the tax regimes such as tax rates, types of taxes and the corporation tax system are not changed. Hence, by setting all of the elements of the tax bases equal to each other, it is possible to identify the effect of the existing rules for the determination of taxable income on the level and the dispersion of the EATR. We compare the EATR of each simulation to the results obtained in the existing tax systems (base case). The rules of the existing tax regimes are described in more detail in section 2.1.2.2.1 above.

(1) Common depreciation on intangibles

We start with the rules for capital allowances in order to examine their impact on the tax base. First we have assumed a common depreciation rate on intangibles which was set by the straight-line method over the estimated period of economic use of 5 years. Since the depreciation of intangibles is already broadly similar in all countries except for the UK, which allows the use of a 25% declining balance pool method, it is not surprising that harmonising these rules has almost no effect on the average EATR and the standard deviation.[50]

(2) Common depreciation on buildings

Harmonising the depreciation on buildings – we have assumed the straight-line method over 25 years in each country – also only has a minor impact on the EATR and the standard deviation. Only three countries are affected by this measure. France's increasing EATR is indicative of its current generous capital allowances on buildings. By contrast, the decreasing EATR of Germany and the Netherlands signal disadvantageous country practices. The minor changes of the EATR indicate that rules regarding the depreciation of buildings are already broadly similar throughout the EU-5 Member States.

---

50 Since we only consider intangibles acquired from third parties, the results could be different for self-created intangibles and for goodwill.

Table 16: Results for simulations of reforming elements of the corporation tax base
- Effective average tax rates
- Only corporate taxes

	FRA	GER	IRL	NL	UK	EU-5 Average	EU-5 Stand. Dev.	USA
Base case	39.7	30.1	8.3	24.0	21.0	24.6	10.4	29.7
1. Common depreciation on intangibles	39.7	30.1	8.3	24.0	21.0	24.6	10.4	29.7
2. Common depreciation on buildings	40.2	29.3	8.3	23.6	21.0	24.5	10.4	28.8
3. Common SL depreciation on tangible fixed assets	44.1	30.6	8.4	24.5	21.4	25.8	11.7	32.3
4. Common DB depreciation on tangible fixed assets	41.0	28.4	7.9	22.3	19.7	23.9	10.9	29.8
5. Common valuation of inventories	38.0	29.7	7.9	21.8	19.2	23.3	10.1	27.5
6. Common pension scheme (book reserve)	44.5	30.1	9.2	27.1	24.0	27.0	11.3	34.1
7. Common pension scheme (pension fund)	39.7	26.2	8.3	24.0	21.0	23.8	10.1	29.7
8. Common book reserves for bad debts	36.2	26.6	7.9	21.4	18.8	22.2	9.3	26.6
9. Common overall tax base (IAS)	46.7	29.7	8.7	24.5	21.4	26.2	12.4	32.3

(3), (4)Common depreciation on tangible fixed assets

With respect to the depreciation on tangible fixed assets – the model firm of the European Tax Analyzer covers 5 different types of machines plus furniture and fixtures – two different scenarios are considered: (3) straight-line over the estimated periods of economic use varying between 5 and 10 years and (4) declining balance at 3 times straight-line over the estimated periods of economic use, at a maximum of 30%. In the case of a common *straight-line depreciation* EATR is increases in each country. The increase is highest in France (4.4 percentage points) and lowest in Ireland (0.1 percentage points). Both the EU-5 average EATR (1.2 percentage points) and the standard deviation (1.3) increase. By contrast, applying a common *30% declining balance depreciation* tends to increase the EATR only in France. In all other countries, we see a decreasing EATR. The EU-5 average EATR also decreases by 0.7 percentage points. However, as with the straight-line method, the standard deviation increases, but only by 0.5.

Several conclusions can be drawn from these results. First, with respect to the changes in the national EATR, it is evident that depreciation practices on tangible fixed assets are still quite different throughout the EU-5 Member States. France seems to be in a relatively favourable position and Ireland in a relatively disadvantageous position. Second, with respect to the level of changes of both the national EATR and the EU-5 average EATR, the different depreciation rules on tangible fixed assets have a considerable impact on the effective tax burdens. This can also be explained by the high weights of tangible fixed assets as a portion the total investment of the model firm. Third, with respect to the increases in the standard deviations, it is evident that common methods and allowance rates for tangible fixed assets would increase differences in the EATR between countries if all other elements of the tax regimes remained unchanged.

(5) Common valuation of inventories

With respect to the valuation of inventories, we have assumed that production costs are valued at *full costs* and that *LIFO* is allowed as an allocation method in each country. This harmonisation scenario tends to decrease all national EATRs and the EU-5 average EATR (by 1.3 percentage points) as well as the standard deviation (by 0.3). Since the explanation of this result has already been given in section 2.1.2.2.1 above, it is only briefly summarised here: full cost tends to increase the tax burden and LIFO tends to decrease the tax burden. Obviously, for our base case model firm, the increasing effect of applying full costs is more than compensated for by the decreasing effect of applying LIFO allocation. Moreover, the calculation of production costs on a full cost basis tends to smooth the differences between different capital allowances and other elements of the production costs (such as pension costs) if the finished goods are stored for a certain period of time. This explains the decrease of the standard deviation.

(6), (7) Common allocation of pension costs

The harmonisation of occupational pension schemes' allocation of pension costs considers two different scenarios: (6) a common regime for building up a pension reserve (book reserve) as in Germany and (7) a common regime for a funded system that allows the deduction of annual (periodical) payments to a pension fund as prevails in the Anglo-Saxon countries . In the case of *book reserves*, the national EATR, except in Germany, the EU-5 average EATR (by 2.4 percentage points) and the standard deviation (by 0.9) increase. The reason for this considerable increase is a broader tax base[51] in each country except Germany and the high portion of pension costs in the total costs of the model firm. A common system for pension funds would only affect the position of Germany since it is already applied in the other countries. Therefore, the impact on both the EU-5 average EATR and the standard deviation is only minor.

(8) Common book reserve for bad debts

It is always very arbitrary to specify conditions under which bad debts occur. Therefore, we did not consider bad debts in our base case at all. The European Tax Analyzer model, however, enables us to account for bad debts. To analyse the effect of such provisions on the tax burden, we now allow the build-up of a book reserve for bad debts in all countries. In doing so we have assumed future warranties which amount to 2% of the annual turnover of the model firm and have to be fulfilled in no later than two years. Accounting for a book reserve for bad debts under these conditions decreases both the national EATR and the EU-5 average EATR (by 2.4 percentage points). The decrease is highest in France and Germany (3.5 percentage points) and lowest in Ireland (0.4 percentage points). This result clearly reflects the (corporation) tax savings due to the deduction of the annual contributions to the book reserve from the tax base. The amount of tax saving increases with the statutory tax rate on profits, which is highest in France (40%) and Germany (39.3%) and lowest in Ireland (10%). The asymmetric decrease of the national EATR is also reflected by the lower standard deviation (9.3 compared to 10.4 in the base case). As a general conclusion from this example, it seems likely that both the national EATR level as well as the dispersion of the EATR across countries are lower compared to the base case if book reserves for bad debts are taken into account. However, with respect to the extreme assumptions in our example – the bad debts amount to 2% of the annual turnover –a considerable variation of the EATR still remains.

---

[51] See section 2.1.2.2.1 above for details.

(9) Common overall tax base (IAS)

In order to get a better idea about the impact of the corporation tax base on the EATR compared to other elements of a tax regime that constitute the effective tax burden (i.e. tax rates, local taxes, corporation tax system), we finally consider a harmonisation scenario with a uniform tax base in all countries. In doing so, we assume that the provisions of the International Accounting Standards (IAS) form, without exception, the basis for the determination of taxable profits in the six countries.[52] In particular, we considered the following rules as simultaneously relevant:[53]

- Depreciation of intangibles, buildings and tangible fixed assets only on a straight-line basis over the estimated periods of economic use – 5 years for intangibles, 40 and 50 years for buildings and 5 to 10 years for tangible fixed assets.

- Valuation of inventories is based on the full costs with FIFO as the allocation method.

- Costs for occupational pension schemes are deducted from the annual taxable profits according to a funded scheme as prevails in the Anglo-Saxon countries.[54]

- Provisions for bad debts are not permitted.

The results presented in Table 16 indicate that, with the exception of Germany, the national EATR would rise if the IAS were relevant for the determination of taxable profits. As a consequence, the EU-5 average EATR increases by 1.6 percentage points. Thus, by taking the IAS as a benchmark, we can conclude that the national accounting provisions are currently more generous. However, since the changes in the EATR in Germany, Ireland, the Netherlands and the UK are only minor, it is only France that seems to be in a relatively favourable position with respect to the tax base. Therefore, the change in the EU-5 average EATR can be above all attributed to the large change in France. As far as the Anglo-Saxon countries and the Netherlands are concerned, the minor changes of the EATR can be attributed to the fact that the tax bases in these countries already correspond to the IAS to a greater extent than the tax bases in European continental states (e.g. France), with an exception made for the USA. Germany's result also suggests that the tax base corresponds with the IAS. Since the German EATR decreases, the

---

52 There is an increasing impact of the IAS on the European Accounting Directive. See, for example, Monti (1998), Ruhnke, Schmidt and Seidel (2000), Seifert (2000). This can also have a considerable impact on the corporation tax base if the determination of taxable income is linked with the accounting standards. This situations prevails in many EU Member States. For an overview see, for example, Hölscher (1999).

53 For more details see Oestreicher and Spengel (1999).

54 See section 2.1.2.2.1 above for details.

national tax accounting rules are even a bit less generous. Although the broadening of the tax base according to international standards was one of the aims of the German tax reform (see Kommission zur Reform der Unternehmensbesteuerung, 1999: 22), this conclusion is misleading. In fact, a lot of differences, which would compensate for each other considerably if the IAS became relevant, still exist.[55] However, with respect to these compensating effects, it is also clear that it is not sufficient just to compare the individual elements of the tax bases (e.g. depreciation rules or provisions) when analysing the impact of the tax bases on the effective tax burden. If the most important elements of the tax bases were included in the comparison, the resulting effects on the effective tax burden could be lower than one might generally expect.

The most striking result of this harmonisation scenario is, however, the increasing standard deviation (by 2.0) which is greater than in all previous simulations. This indicates that with a harmonised overall corporation tax base the differences between the national EATR would not only remain, but that these differences would even increase since the variation in the EATR across countries increases. The remaining variations in the EATR can be attributed to the different statutory tax rates, local taxes and the corporation tax systems. In the case of a uniform tax base, the real effects resulting solely from these differences are clearly demonstrated. As pointed out earlier in section 2, the corporation tax seems to be designed as a whole: higher tax rates tend to be combined with lower tax bases and vice versa (see Table 10 above). This correlation might explain the increasing dispersion of the EATR when tax bases are harmonised: in such instances the compensating element (i.e. a more generous tax base) disappears.

6.3 Reforming the corporation tax rates and the local taxes

This report considers 4 simulations listed in Part B of Box 2 which refer to corporation tax rates and local taxes. In order to separately identify the impact of the relevant provisions on the EATR, we again consider single elements of the tax rates as well as combinations of the corporation tax rate and local taxes. The results of each simulation are listed in Table 17 and compared with the results obtained from the existing tax systems (base case). The rules of the existing tax systems are described in more detail in section 2.1.2.2.2 above.

---

55 We are just referring to the valuation of inventories – partial costs and average cost allocation – and the allocation of pension costs – book reserves – described in section 2.1.2.2.1 above. Therefore, the changes of the EATR could be different for different branches or industries. See Oestreicher and Spengel (1999).

Table 17: Results for simulations of reforming tax rates and local taxes
- Effective average tax rates
- Only corporate taxes

	FRA	GER	IRL	NL	UK	EU-5 Average	EU-5 Stand. Dev.	USA
Base case	39.7	30.1	8.3	24.0	21.0	24.6	10.4	29.7
10. Common CT rate, at EU mean	36.7	34.1	23.6	21.8	22.7	27.8	6,3	28.4
11. Common CT rate incl. local profit taxes, at EU mean	37.1	24.0	24.5	23.1	24.0	26.5	5.3	25.3
12. Common CT rate of 25% incl. local profit taxes	33.6	17.0	18.3	16.6	17.5	20.6	6.5	19.7
13. Common CT rate of 25% incl. all local taxes	9.6	17.0	16.2	16.2	14.8	14.8	2.7	16.2

(10) Common corporation tax rate, including surcharges, without local taxes, rate at EU average

This reform scenario introduces a common corporation tax rate of 32.28% including all surcharges levied in France and Germany. The rate of 32.28% is the average rate across all 15 EU Member States, except for Germany where we have already referred to the situation after the tax reform in 2001, for the fiscal year 1999. However, this simulation does not imply that in all Member States all profits will be taxed at the same rates. Since local profit taxes are still levied – in our country sample it is the German trade tax and the US franchise tax on income – differences will remain. Moreover, all countries still levy local non-profit taxes.

Introducing such a common corporation tax rate increases the EU-5 average EATR significantly, by 3.2 percentage points. At the same time, however, there is also a considerable reduction of the standard deviation from 10.4 to 6.3 indicating less variation of the EATR across EU Member States. In fact, since the EATR does not change significantly in France, the Netherlands and the UK, these changes are mainly caused by Germany and Ireland. The EATR in Germany increases by 4.0 percentage points. Since there is an extra burden imposed by the trade tax on income in Germany, the statutory tax rate on profits would rise from 39.3% to 44.2%.[56] However, the most significant change is in Ireland with an increase of the EATR by 15.3 percentage points from 8.3% to 23.6%. This is because the advantage of the 10% corporation tax rate now would disappear.

It should be noted that – in contrast to all simulations considering the tax base – the ranking of the countries would be different from the base case. Ireland would drop back from first to third place whereas the Netherlands would improve from third to first place. The other countries would keep their positions. Since only the corporation tax rate is harmonised, this country ranking reflects the remaining differences between the effects of the tax bases, the local profit and non-profit taxes and the corporation tax systems.

(11) Common corporation tax rate, including surcharges and local profit taxes, without local non-profit taxes, rate at EU average

This simulation is based on the previous one, but now local profit taxes are included in the common statutory tax rate. For our sample of countries this implies that the trade tax in Germany and the franchise tax on income in the USA are assumed to be abolished, or alternatively, credited against corporation tax.[57] For the uniform tax rate we have chosen 33.84%, which represents the average statutory tax rate across the 15 EU Member States.

Since only Germany levies a local profit tax within the EU-5 Member States, this harmonisation scenario would significantly reduce the EATR in Germany. By contrast, there would only be moderate increases of the EATR in the other countries. Germany would improve two positions to second place, bringing it to a level equal to that of the UK. Altogether, the EU-5 average EATR would be reduced moderately and the standard deviation of the EATR across countries would fall further. The new value of 5.3 is almost by 50% lower than the standard deviation of the EATR for the existing tax regimes (base case). Compared to the existing tax regimes, introducing a harmonised statutory tax rate on profits would therefore substantially reduce distortions resulting from differences between the EATR for domestic investment in Europe.

---

56 The corporation tax rate in Germany would rise from 26.38% (see section 4.1) to 32.28%.

57 A statutory tax rate on profits, including local profit taxes, was recommended, for example, by the Ruding Committee. See Commission of the European Communities (1992: 219). In fact, in Germany the trade tax is credited against income tax on trading income. However, the trade tax is not credited against corporation tax in Germany.

However, not all distortions would disappear. The remaining differences can be attributed to the tax bases, the local non-profit taxes and the corporation tax systems. France in particular, would still be in a very disadvantageous position with respect to the levy of non-profit taxes.

(12) Common corporation tax rate at 25%, including surcharges and local profit taxes, without local non-profit taxes

Compared to the previous case, this simulation simply reduces the common statutory tax rate on profits from the EU average rate of 33.84% to 25%. As a consequence of the lower tax rate all of the national EATRs as well as the EU-5 average EATR would be further reduced. However, with respect to the increasing standard deviation, the more striking result of this simulation is that the dispersion of the EATR rises. This happens because the tax saving due to the deductibility of local non-profit taxes becomes smaller as the statutory tax rate on profits decreases. In other words, the effects of the different non-profit tax levels emerge more obviously if the statutory tax rate on profits is reduced.

The result of this simulation is also important since it reveals the effects of the tax rate on the variation of the effective tax burdens. The comparison with the previous simulation makes clear that a further reduction of a statutory tax rate on profits, which is already harmonised, to a level significantly lower than the average across countries, will only reduce the average effective tax burden. However, the economic distortion will increase, since the standard deviation rises.

(13) Common corporation tax rate at 25%, including surcharges and all local profit and non-profit taxes

In addition to measures considered in the previous case, this simulation abolishes non-profit taxes (e.g. real property tax). This implies that the only tax that exists in each country is an income tax on profits which is levied at a uniform rate of 25%. Since there are no other taxes, the remaining differences between the EATR are the result of the different tax bases and the corporation tax systems. As a result of this simulation, all of the national EATRs and the EU-5 average EATR would be further reduced. Moreover, the standard deviation of the EATR is falls to 2.7, by far the lowest value obtained in any of the 15 simulations.

At first glance, this harmonisation scenario does not seem very realistic. However, one should consider the development in the past which highlighted a clear trend towards the abolition of non-profit taxes and a reduction in the statutory tax rate on profits (see section 5 for details). Even if the near future does not end up with overall tax rates of 25%, this scenario illuminates the remaining dispersions of the effective tax burdens across countries which can be attributed to the tax bases and the corporation tax systems. Furthermore, with reference to our results, these dispersions are lower as could be expected.

In the country ranking France moves from last to first position. But this result is not surprising, since France has the lowest tax base (see Table 10) and is the only country that uses an imputation system.

6.4 Reforming the corporation tax systems

In the past decade, much of the debate on co-ordinating and harmonising company taxation in Europe has been focused on the corporation tax systems. The debate over corporation tax systems deals with the relationship between corporate and personal income taxes. In section 2.2 the fact that the role of personal taxes with respect to investment and location decisions of companies is not clear was discussed. Personal taxes might be less important for multinationals than for small and medium-sized companies. Moreover, with respect to the fundamental freedoms of the EC Treaty there has been heavy pressure on imputation systems. The abolition of the UK partial imputation system (see Gammie, 1997) and the German full imputation system (see Kommission zur Reform der Unternehmensbesteuerung, 1999: 16-17) and the introduction of shareholder relief systems in both countries is a reaction to this dispute. This also follows a clear trend within in the EU.[58]

We do not intend to continue with the discussion about an adequate corporation tax system for Europe here. Instead, we simply want to demonstrate the impact of a common corporation tax system on the level and the dispersion of companies' effective tax burden. For the purposes of simplification, and since there is a trend currently towards the abolition of imputation systems, we have chosen the classical system. All other elements of the tax regimes remained the same. Since the corporation tax system is the linkage between corporate and personal income taxes, we have introduced personal taxes in a separate step. In the case of personal taxes, the amount of dividends is the same as in the base case (see section 1.4) and there is no "shareholder relief" on dividend income. The results are listed in Table 18.

58 See section 5 and more generally Jacobs (1999: 125-128).

Table 18: Results for corporation tax system reform simulations
- Effective average tax rates
- Corporate and personal taxes

	FRA	GER	IRL	NL	UK	EU-5 Average	EU-5 Stand. Dev.	USA
Base case (only corporate taxes)	39.7	30.1	8.3	24.0	21.0	24.6	10.4	29.7
Base case (corporate and personal taxes)	48.8	31.0	17.2	32.0	25.6	30.9	10.4	32.0
14. Common CT system, classical system (only corporate taxes)	48.0	30.1	8.3	24.0	21.0	26.3	13.0	29.7
15. Common CT system, classical system (corporate and personal taxes)	55.7	32.0	17.2	37.4	26.6	33.8	12.8	32.0

(14) Common corporation tax system, classical system, only corporate taxes

At the corporation level the introduction of a common classical system would only affect the EATR in France. This is because all of the countries considered here except France already apply a kind of classical system at the corporate level.[59] As demonstrated in section 4, which dealt with the German tax reform, the abolition of the imputation system, in general, would increase the EATR. The reason is that if the tax credit is denied, a relatively higher cash distribution will be required to pay the same amount of dividends as before. As a result of the increasing French EATR, both the average EU-5 EATR and the standard deviation of the EATR across countries rises.

[59] In fact, these countries apply the classical system or a kind of shareholder relief system. Since there is no tax credit either in a classical system or in a shareholder relief system, the distinction between these two systems at the corporate level (without taking into account personal taxes) has no consequences.

(15) Common corporation tax system, classical system, corporate and personal taxes

Introducing an EU-wide classical system and including personal taxes would leave only the effective tax burden in Ireland (and in the USA) unaffected. By contrast, since none of these countries operates a pure classical system, the EATR in all other countries would rise. The EATR increase would be most significant in France (from 48.8% to 55.7%) due to its high average income tax rate (see section 2.2). There would be only minor increases in the EATR in Germany and the UK. Altogether, the EU-5 average EATR at the overall level would rise. The same is true for the standard deviation, which increases from 10.4 to 12.8.

To summarise, it seems reasonable to conclude that the introduction of a common corporation tax system without modifying other elements of the tax regimes at the same time would increase distortions, resulting from different levels of company taxation, within the EU. There are different reasons for this result. At the corporation level the effects resulting from the different tax rates, tax bases and local taxes would emerge if there were a common corporation tax system. At the overall level it is the different structure of the income tax rates that increases the variation of the EATR.

6.5 Conclusions

A major finding in sections 2-5 was that all tax regimes are designed as more or less integrated systems. This means that there is a particular relationship between the tax rate, the tax base and the corporation tax system. As a broad conclusion, it is possible to say that, in general, a higher statutory tax rate on profits correlates with a lower taxable base and vice versa. Moreover, compared to an imputation system, the algebraic sum of the statutory tax rate on corporate profits and the (marginal and average) tax rate on capital income at the shareholder's level tends to be lower in a classical, or shareholder relief system, and vice versa. As a result of these particular relationships, it is clear that a neutral tax regime across EU Member States can only be reached by simultaneously strictly harmonising the tax rates, tax bases, taxes and corporation tax systems. However, this option – which is, in fact, a full harmonisation – is not at all feasible or realistic.

Table 19: Summary of simulation results
- Effective average tax rates
- Only corporate taxes

	FRA	GER	IRL	NL	UK	EU-5 Average	EU-5 Stand. Dev.	USA
Base case	39.7	30.1	8.3	24.0	21.0	24.6	10.4	29.7
9. Common overall tax base (IAS)	46.7	29.7	8.7	24.5	21.4	26.2	12.4	32.3
11. Common CT rate incl. local profit taxes, at EU mean	37.1	24.0	24.5	23.1	24.0	26.5	5.3	25.3
14. Common CT system, classical system (only corporate taxes)	48.0	30.1	8.3	24.0	21.0	26.3	13.0	29.7

Instead, from a practical point of view, it is more realistic to put pressure on co-ordinating (or harmonising) only certain elements of the tax regimes. In doing so, it is above all necessary to understand the weights of each of the most important elements of a tax regime in the effective tax burden. Therefore, this section of the report has been aimed at analysing the impact of the different elements of the tax regimes on the effective average tax burden of companies. In particular, the impact of the corporation tax base, the corporation tax rate including surcharges and local taxes, and the corporation tax system have been examined in separate steps. The results of the most important simulations, with respect to corporate taxes, are presented in Table 19.

Introducing a *common corporate tax base* – in simulation (9) we chose International Accounting Standards – clearly helps to achieve more transparency in the calculation of effective tax burdens. Therefore, the dispute about the effects of a generous tax base compared to a relatively low tax rate on the effective tax burden would certainly come to an end. However, the outcome of this simulation indicates that such a change would result in increasing values both for the average effective tax burden in Europe and – what seems more important – the dispersion of the EATR across EU Member States.

Similarly, a *common corporation tax system* – in simulation (14) we chose the classical system – tends to increase both the average effective tax burden in Europe and the dispersion of the EATR across EU Member States.

By contrast, the introduction of a *common statutory tax rate on profits* – in simulation (11) we chose the EU average of 33.84% including surcharges and local profit taxes – would significantly reduce the dispersion of the EATR across the EU Member States. None of the other hypothetical reforms considered here reduced the variation of the effective tax burdens in a comparable way. The effects on the EATR of a common statutory tax rate on profits depends on level of the tax rate. In our example, the average EATR increases. Although a lower common tax rate would reduce the average EATR, the dispersion of the EATR across countries tends to rise again. Therefore, reducing statutory tax rates on profits significantly does not simultaneously ensure greater neutrality towards taxation.

7 Comparison of the European Tax Analyzer results with those obtained by the Devereux-Griffith model

7.1 Problems inherent in comparing results obtained by different approaches

The most meaningful indicators for the measurement of effective levels of company tax burdens are forward-looking concepts. Depending on the type of investment and its return respectively, we can distinguish between the effective marginal and the effective average tax rate. The standard model for the calculation of the effective *marginal* tax rate (EMTR) is the well known approach of King and Fullerton (1984). This approach has been applied in the most important international studies on the effective tax burden of companies in the past decade.[60] By contrast, no standard model exists for the calculation of the effective average tax rate (EATR).

The European Tax Analyzer, which is used in this report, is one alternative approach for the calculation of the EATR. The European Tax Analyzer is based on the model firm approach and simulates the decision making of a potential investor (i.e. a company). The model calculates the impact of different tax regimes on the investor's target figure. The return on equity was chosen as the target figure in this study (see section 2.2) . The Devereux-Griffith (1999) model is another approach for the calculation of the EATR. Devereux and Griffith have extended the model of King and Fullerton in several ways. The most important extension is the inclusion of profitable investments (i.e. investments which generate pure profits or economic rents) which are decisive for the calculation of the EATR. The uniqueness of the Devereux and Griffith model is its ability to simultaneously calculate the EMTR and EATR under the same set of assumptions.

By the time this report is prepared the Devereux-Griffith model will be used in another report on the effective tax burden on companies in Europe. That report is based on exactly the same information about the tax regimes as this report and uses as a basis also information for the fiscal year 1999.[61] In order to see how the effective average tax rates (EATRs) in the EU Member States are influenced by these two different approaches, the results obtained with the European Tax Analyzer are compared with those obtained by the Devereux-Griffith model.

---

60 See, for example, OECD (1991), Commission of the European Communities (1992), Caron & Stevens, Baker & McKenzie (1999).

61 See Devereux, Lammersen and Spengel (2000). The Devereux-Griffith model was also applied in order to analyse the effects of the German tax reform of 2001 in a broader context. See Bond and Chennells (2000).

Although both concepts are meaningful forward-looking concepts, their results will be different with respect to the level of the EATR even if exactly the same tax regime is analysed. There are three main reasons for this divergence.

- *Economic data*: The calculations in both models are based on different assumptions about the economic data. The Devereux-Griffith model assumes a new capital stock, a capital market with identical interest rates and a simpler model of a company that carries out an investment. By contrast, the European Tax Analyzer is based on a more complex model of a hypothetical firm that covers several assets and liabilities which go beyond the scope of assets and liabilities included in the Devereux-Griffith model of. For example, furniture and fixtures or pension liabilities are not included in the current version of the Devereux-Griffith model.[62] Moreover, the European Tax Analyzer model even allows the simulation of used capital stock and split interest rates in the capital market. The latter also implies that the effects of different tax systems on the liquidity (cash flow) can be taken into account without any difficulty.

  The different concepts used in both economic models also imply different weights for the types of assets and the sources of finance as well as different levels of profitability, interest and inflation rates.

  Another important difference between the economic models is the treatment of a corporation's retained earnings. The Devereux-Griffith model assumes that profit retention does affect the capital gains taxes of private investors. The European Tax Analyzer is based on a different assumption: that no capital gains are realised since retained earnings can be distributed as dividends in later periods.

- *Tax data*: Both models are based on different assumptions about the tax variables. The Devereux-Griffith model only takes exogenous tax rate structures into account. By contrast, the European Tax Analyzer model considers progressive tax rates, allowances for certain categories of income or for certain types of tax payers and, since more assets and liabilities are included in the economic model, more elements of the tax base (accounting provisions) such as the calculation of production costs or allocation of pension costs.

- *EATR calculation method*: The EATRs are calculated in technically different ways. Whereas the EATR in the Devereux-Griffith model is expressed in terms of the change of the net present value of the firm, the European Tax Analyzer expresses the EATR in terms of the change of the value of the firm at the end of the simulation period (see section 2.2).

---

62 Since the Devereux-Griffith model could include more assets and liabilities, this is not a methodological limitation of their approach. It just explains why the results of the present studies may differ.

The remainder of this section compares the results of the base case scenarios as well as the effects of the German tax reform 2001 and the simulations on tax harmonisation. The comparison is only made for the five EU Member States dealt with in this report (France, Germany, Ireland, the Netherlands and the UK). Moreover, the comparison deals only with domestic investment and excludes the USA.

7.2 Comparison of the effective tax burdens for the base case scenarios

7.2.1 Level of the corporation

The comparison is made in two stages. First, we consider only the taxes at the corporation level. Afterwards, personal taxes will be included. Each stage takes four measures for the tax burden into account:

- the overall statutory tax rate on profits (i.e. including local profit taxes like the trade tax in Germany),
- the effective *marginal* tax rates (EMTR) calculated with the Devereux-Griffith model ,
- the effective average tax rates (EATR) calculated with the Devereux-Griffith model and
- the effective average tax rates (EATR) calculated with the European Tax Analyzer in this report.

The joint comparison of the different tax burden measures' results presented in Table 20 reveals the following results:

- The effective tax burden – irrespective whether it is a marginal (EMTR) or an average (EATR) indicator – always ranges below the statutory tax rate on profits. Since the statutory tax rate on profits does not take the effects of the tax bases into account, the consideration of the rules for income determination thus generally causes the effective tax burden to range below the statutory tax rate.
- Except for Ireland and the UK, the EMTR is below the EATR. This can be explained by the fact that the impact of the tax bases on the EATR decreases as profitability increases. Therefore, the EATR tends to converge to the statutory tax rate.[63] The higher values of the EMTR compared with the EATR

---

63 For further explanation see Devereux and Griffith (1999), Devereux, Lammersen and Spengel (2000).

in Ireland and the UK can be attributed to the relatively high portion of non-profit taxes in both countries (i.e. real property tax or business rates, see Table 5 above) combined with a relatively low statutory tax rate on profits.

Table 20: Comparison of statutory tax rates, effective marginal tax rates and effective average tax rates across 5 EU Member States - Only corporate taxes

	Statutory tax rate %	EMTR[a)] %	EATR %		
			Devereux-Griffith[b)] (1)	European Tax Analyzer[c)] (2)	Difference (1)-(2) in %
FRA	40.0	33.2	37.5	39.7	-5.5
GER	52.3	31.0	39.1	32.8	19.2
IRL	10.0	11.7	10.5	8.3	26.5
NL	35.0	22.6	31.0	24.0	29.2
UK	30.0	24.7	28.2	21.0	34.3

a) and b) See Devereux, Lammersen and Spengel (2000), Appendix D

c) See Table 4 in this report

Finally, the comparison of the two average indicators reveals, that the EATR calculated with the Devereux-Griffith model is, in general, higher than the EATR calculated with the European Tax Analyzer model. The only exception in our sample is France. However, this can be simply explained by the fact that, in contrast to the Devereux-Griffith model, a higher portion of French non-profit taxes is included in the European Tax Analyzer. The three "employer taxes" and the personnel expenses forming part of the base of the "taxe professionnelle" are included in the European Tax Analyzer. There could be several reasons for the other four countries' lower EATR as calculated with the European Tax Analyzer model. Since these reasons were explained above, they will only be repeated here: the use of different economic and tax data as well as a technically different method for calculating the EATR. Since the proportional distances between both EATRs presented in the last two columns of Table 20 vary for each country, it seems reasonable to conclude that it is not possible to make any universally valid conclusion about the EATR level in a particular country or the differences in the EATR between countries.

The most striking result of the comparison is, however, that with the exception of France and Germany, the ranking of the countries from the highest to the lowest EATR is the same for each model. According to these results, France and Germany have the highest EATR while Ireland has by far the lowest EATR.

Moreover, this EATR country ranking closely follows the country ranking according to statutory tax rates. For the Devereux-Griffith model, the ranking of the EATR even corresponds exactly to the ranking of the statutory tax rates. Therefore, the broad conclusions that were drawn for the base cases in both reports do not seem to be affected. Considering the elements of the tax regimes that have a significant impact on the effective tax burden at the corporation level, it is above all the statutory tax rates that can explain the levels and the differences of the EATRs. With respect to the situation in France, the local non-profit taxes might also have a considerable impact on the EATR. The effects of the different tax bases however, are only minor.

7.2.2 Overall level (corporation and domestic shareholders)

The results of the comparison of the tax burdens at the overall level including personal taxes are presented in Table 21. In this Table, the statutory tax rate corresponds to the marginal income tax rate including surcharges (such as, for example, the solidarity levy in Germany). The effective marginal and the effective average tax rates calculated with the Devereux-Griffith model are an unweighted average for the zero-rated, top-rate non-qualified and top-rate qualified shareholders included in this model. The European Tax Analyzer results are those for the base case, which considers 10 shareholders in a medium-sized corporation.

Table 21: Comparison of statutory tax rates, effective marginal tax rates and effective average tax rates across 5 EU Member States
- Corporate and personal taxes

	Statutory tax rate %	EMTR[a] %	EATR %		
			Devereux-Griffith[b] (1)	European Tax Analyzer[c] (2)	Difference (1)-(2) in %
FRA	61.3	60.8	39.5	48.8	-19.1
GER	55.9	58.1	37.7	37.4	0.1
IRL	46.0	41.5	27.1	17.2	57.6
NL	60.0	71.5	38.3	32.0	19.7
UK	40.0	46.9	33.2	25.6	29.7

a) and b) Unweighted averages across three types of shareholders. See Devereux, Lammersen and Spengel (2000), Appendix D, own calculations

c) See Table 11 in this report

The comparison of the statutory tax rates with the effective tax rates is less clear than it was at the corporation level. The EMTR is higher than the statutory tax rate in three countries (Germany, the Netherlands and the UK), whereas in two countries (France and Ireland), it is slightly lower. There are several reasons for this result. Since the EMTR was not calculated in this report, the following only summarises the most important reasons for these differences. In addition to effects that were already relevant for the corporation level tax burden , this result is affected by the corporation tax systems, the personal tax rates levied on different categories of capital income and the imposition of private property taxes. Any corporation tax system different from a full imputation system tends to raise the EMTR above the statutory tax rate. The same is true in case of private property taxes and if capital gains upon the disposal of shares are subject to personal income taxation (i.e. capital gains tax). By contrast, the fact that capital income is often taxed at reduced rates and that the effective tax burden in the Devereux-Griffith model is an average figure, including up to one third of the zero-rated shareholders,[64] tends to push the EMTR below the statutory tax rate. For further details about the EMTR we refer to the other report using the Devereux-Griffith model (see Devereux, Lammersen and Spengel, 2000).

In contrast to the corporation level, both average indicators for each country are below the statutory tax rate and the EMTR. The main reason for this result is the existence of pure profits (economic rents) and the way these profits are taxed in the models. In the event of pure profits, the weight of non-profit taxes at the shareholder's level (e.g. private property taxes which tend to be high in France and the Netherlands) is reduced. Moreover, the pure profits at the corporation level are taxed at a first stage. After deducting corporate taxes the profits can either be distributed as dividends or retained by the corporation.[65] In many countries dividends and retained earnings bear a lower tax burden compared to alternative sources of capital income Therefore the assumptions of both models tend to further reduce the EATR.

Finally, as at the corporation level, the EATR at the overall level calculated with the European Tax Analyzer tends to be lower than the EATR calculated with the Devereux-Griffith model. Again, the only exception is France. The reasons for this result are basically the same as for the corporation level. Therefore, we refer to the above analysis. Moreover, since the European Tax Analyzer does not simply use the marginal income tax rates, but instead endogenously calculates average income tax rates according to the progressive tariffs, this also tends to reduce the EATR when compared with the Devereux-Griffith model.

---

64 Zero-rated shareholders are not necessarily included in the Devereux-Griffith model.

65 In the Devereux-Griffith model, all economic rents are distributed as dividends to the ultimate shareholder. In the European Tax Analyzer, the profits can also be retained by the corporation.

Again, however, the most striking result is that the country ranking according to the EATR is almost the same for the two approaches. According to this ranking, France has the highest and Ireland the lowest EATR. Therefore, the broad conclusions for the base case are not affected by the methodological approach.[66]

7.3 Effects of the German tax reform 2001

Both reports prepared for the European Commission take the tax regimes which were in force in the fiscal year 1999 as a base. However, the effects of the German tax reform which becomes effective as of January 1, 2001, are considered in separate sections. In principal, the calculations in both reports take into account the same set of tax changes:[67]

- *Corporation tax system*: Abolition of the full imputation system and introduction of a shareholder relief system in which only one half of the dividends received by a private shareholder are subject to personal income tax.
- *Tax rates*: Reduction of the corporation tax rate from 40% (for retained earnings) and 30% (for distributed profits) to 25% and reduction of the marginal personal income tax rate from 53% to 42% up by the year 2005.
- *Corporation tax base*: Reduction of the declining balance depreciation rate for tangible fixed assets from 30% to 20% and of the straight-line depreciation rate for buildings from 4% to 3%.

Although the other report which uses the Devereux-Griffith model also took the effects of the German tax reform on the effective marginal tax rate into account, the following comparison concentrates on the effective average tax rates. Table 22 lists the results of the two reports for the corporation level and the overall level including personal taxes.

---

66 The different position of the Netherlands can be explained by the fact that under the European Tax Analyzer's assumptions the more favourable shareholder relief always applies for the taxation of dividend income. By contrast, in the Devereux-Griffith model, the disadvantageous classical system is applied to non-qualified shareholders. The Dutch corporation tax system is described in more detail in section 2.2.2 above. The relatively low overall EATR for Ireland in the European Tax Analyzer is explained by the low distribution rate in the base case. Therefore, since most of the profits are retained by the corporation, a high portion of profits benefits from the 10% manufacturing relief.

67 See section 4 in this report and section 6 in Devereux, Lammersen and Spengel (2000).

Table 22: Effective average tax rate in Germany before and after the reform
- Comparison of Devereux-Griffith and European Tax Analyzer results
- Corporate and personal taxes

	Statutory tax rate %	EMTR[a)] %	EATR %		
			Devereux-Griffith[b)] (1)	European Tax Analyzer[c)] (2)	Difference (1)-(2) in %
Corporate level					
GER 1999	52.3	31.0	39.1	32.8	19.2
GER 2001	39.3	26.0	34.8	30.1	15.6
Overall level					
GER 1999	55.9	58.1	37.7	37.4	0.1
GER 2001	44.3	45.6	36.2	30.1	20.3

a) and b) Unweighted averages across three types of shareholders. See Devereux, Lammersen and Spengel (2000), Appendix D and F, own calculations

c) See Table 15in this report

In both models the German tax reform reduces the EATR. However, there are different degrees of reduction. At the corporation level, the reduction is higher if the Devereux-Griffith model is used (–11% compared to –8.2%). By contrast, at the overall level, the European Tax Analyzer model calculates a significantly higher reduction (–19.5% compared to –4%). At the corporation level, the difference above all is explained by different weights for the assets and sources of finance as well as by the different treatment of the changes of the corporation tax system.[68] The higher reduction of the EATR for the overall level in the European Tax Analyzer model can simply be attributed to the different categories of shareholders that were taken into account for the calculations. The result for the Devereux-Griffith model is an unweighted average for three different categories of shareholders including zero-rated shareholders. By contrast, the European Tax

68 In our European Tax Analyzer approach, the denial of the corporation tax credit in the new German shareholder relief system increases the corporation's tax burden (since it is assumed that a higher distribution is necessary to pay the same amount of dividends, see section 4), in the Devereux-Griffith model, the shareholders' tax burden is increased. However, in both approaches, the relationship between the corporation tax and the personal income tax could also be modelled in the same way.

Analyzer takes only the 10 shareholders in the base case into account. Since these 10 shareholders are close to top rate shareholders, they benefit from a relatively high tax reduction after the reform. The situation could be different and closer to the results of the Devereux-Griffith model, however, if we considered a larger number of shareholders (see section 4.3 and Figure 8 above).

The most important result from the comparison however, is that irrespective of the methodological approach, Germany does not gain more than one position in the country ranking. At the corporation level, Germany moves from the first to the second highest place if the Devereux-Griffith model is used. There are no changes in the European Tax Analyzer model. At the overall level, Germany moves from the second to the third highest place if the European Tax Analyzer model is used. Therefore, the broad conclusions on the quantitative effects of the German tax reform 2001 with respect to domestic investment do not seem to be restricted by the methodology used for the calculation of the effective average tax rate:

- The German tax reform is an important reform since it simultaneously changes the corporation tax system, the tax rates and the tax base.
- There is a significant reduction of the EATR for domestic investment in Germany.
- There are, however, only minor improvements for Germany in the ranking of the EU Member States from the highest to the lowest corporation level EATR. Compared to the other countries, the corporation level EATR is still high. Depending on the structure of the shareholders there might be, however, a considerable improvement at the overall level.

7.4 Effects of hypothetical tax reforms in the EU

In order to identify and analyse the impact of the different elements of the tax regimes on the effective tax burden, both reports consider a number of hypothetical tax reforms. In the following, we compare the results of the most important simulations with respect to domestic investment. In particular, these simulations deal with the impact of a reform on the corporation tax base, the corporation tax rate and the corporation tax system. The relevant simulations of the two reports cover the following tax rules:

Corporation tax base: Both reports consider a common corporation tax base. In this report, the International Accounting Standards were chosen (see section 6.2 for details). In the report using the Devereux-Griffith model, a common depreciation on machinery (declining balance at 2 times straight-line over 7 years), buildings (straight-line over 25 years) and intangibles (straight-line over 7 years) as well as a common valuation of inventories (LIFO) were taken into account.

- Corporation tax rate: Both reports considered a common statutory tax rate on profits at the EU average of 33.84% including surcharges and local profit taxes.

- Corporation tax system: Both reports consider the classical system as a common corporation tax system.[69]

Table 23 presents the results of the two reports for the three simulations and – for the sake of comparison – the results for the base cases. Moreover, Table 23 presents the average EATRs and the standard deviations across the 5 EU Member States covered by this report. Since the other report which uses the Devereux-Griffith model covers all EU-Member States, we also present average EATRs and standard deviations for all 15 EU Member States.

The effects of both models on the EATRs are not the exactly the same in the simulations of a common tax base and of a common tax system. In addition to the fundamental differences between the two approaches explained in the first Chapter of this section, these differences can be attributed to different assumptions for modelling the simulations. In the event of a common tax base, the scope and the type of tax rules clearly differ in both models. With respect to the common tax system, the different result for France is explained by the fact, that the European Tax Analyzer model assumes that the denial of the corporation tax credit which is caused by the change from the full imputation to the classical system increases the corporation tax burden. However, the results concerning the simulation of a common tax rate have exactly the same effects on the national EATRs and the EU average EATR.

Again, the most important result from the comparison with respect to the standard deviations is, that irrespective of the methodological approach, the introduction of a common statutory tax rate on profits would be qualified as the most efficient measure to reduce the dispersion of the EATRs across countries. Since the standard deviation based on the results of the European Tax Analyzer is considerably higher than the one based on the results of the Devereux-Griffith model, it is possible that the impact of the tax bases is underestimated in the Devereux-Griffith model. The reason for this difference may stem from the fact that the Devereux-Griffith model covers fewer elements of the bases than the European Tax Analyzer. However, it seems more likely that the higher standard deviations derived from the results of the European Tax Analyzer model have to be attributed to the relatively high French EATR. Moreover, it should be stressed, however, that the general conclusions that are drawn from the results of the simulations do not seem to be affected by the model in use for the calculation of the EATRs.

---

69 In the other report, the implications of imputation systems and shareholder relief systems were also analysed.

Table 23: Summary of simulation results
- Comparison of Devereux-Griffith and European Tax Analyzer results
- Effective average tax rates
- Only corporate taxes

	FRA	GER	IRL	NL	UK	EU-5 Average	EU-5 Stand. Dev.	EU-15 Average	EU-15 Stand. Dev.
Base case Devereux-Griffith	37.5	34.8	10.5	31.0	28.2	28.4	9.5	29.2	6.1
European Tax Analyzer	39.7	30.1	8.3	24.0	21.0	24.6	10.4	n.a.	n.a.
Common overall tax base Devereux-Griffith	37.9	34.7	10.0	30.3	27.4	28.1	9.7	29.2	6.3
European Tax Analyzer	46.7	29.7	8.7	24.5	21.4	26.2	12.4	n.a.	n.a.
Common CT rate incl. Local profit taxes, at EU mean Devereux-Griffith	32.6	29.4	31.5	30.0	31.5	31.0	1.2	30.0	1.2
European Tax Analyzer	37.1	24.0	24.5	23.1	24.0	26.5	5.3	n.a.	n.a.
Common CT system, classical system Devereux-Griffith	37.5	34.8	10.5	31.0	28.2	28.4	9.5	29.2	6.1
European Tax Analyzer	48.0	30.1	8.3	24.0	21.0	26.3	13.0	n.a.	n.a.

Note: For the results of the Devereux-Griffith model see Devereux, Lammersen and Spengel (2000), Appendix G and own calculations. For the results of the European Tax Analyzer see Table 19 in this report

7.5 Conclusions

Different models exist for the calculation of companies' effective average tax burden. The final section of this report has compared the results derived by the European Tax Analyzer in this report with the results derived by the Devereux-Griffith model. The latter approach was applied in a parallel report for the European Commission on the same subject.

The two approaches differ with respect to their economic models, the tax variables included in the models and the techniques for calculating the EATR. Therefore, it is almost impossible to arrive at the same EATR even in the event of an identical tax regime.

Nonetheless, the comparison of the most important results computed for domestic investment revealed that neither the main conclusions in this report nor in the other report based on the Devereux-Griffith model are affected by the methodology to a great extent. This was shown for the base case scenario, the effects of the German tax reform 2001 and the implications of a number of hypothetical tax reforms.

8 Final conclusion

This report has presented estimates for the effective average tax rate (EATR) on domestic investment in five EU Member States (France, Germany, Ireland, the Netherlands and the UK) and the USA.

The main aim of the study was to compute and compare EATR on investment by a domestic company in different locations. A secondary aim was to work out the impact of the different tax drivers on the effective tax burden, i.e. to show how the EATR is influenced by the tax systems, the different types of (profit and non-profit) taxes, the tax bases and the tax rates.

The computation and comparison of the EATRs was based on the European Tax Analyzer model. The European Tax Analyzer is a computer based model firm approach for the computation and comparison of international company tax burdens. Since the model firm is designed as a corporation, the tax burden can be calculated at the level of the corporation as well as at the level of the shareholders. The EATR is derived by simulating the development of a corporation over a ten year period. For the computation of the tax burden the model took into account the most relevant and complex provisions of the tax regimes.

The comparison of the EATRs for a typical medium-sized corporation as well as various sensitivity analyses for alternative assumptions of both economic and tax data revealed a wide spread between the effective tax burden in different EU Member States. The levels of the EATRs and the differences between EU Member States depend on individual circumstances of a company such as, for example, profitability, types of investment and sources of finance. It has been shown that the tax regimes can distort competition with respect to location, financing and investment decisions to a considerable extent. Although the differences between the national EATR declined in the past, tax driven distortions have not disappeared.

These distortions are the result of the different types of taxes, tax rates, tax bases and corporation tax systems. It could be worked out in sensitivity analyses and simulations of hypothetical tax reforms that from these elements of a tax regime the statutory tax rate on profits in general has the highest impact on the level of the EATR and the differences between the EATRs across EU Member States. This result is confirmed by other meaningful approaches for the computation of the effective tax burden of companies.

References

Arbeitskreis "Betriebliche Pensionsfonds" (1998), *Bericht des Arbeitskreises "Betriebliche Pensionsfonds" im Auftrag des "Forums Finanzplatz" beim Bundesministerium der Finanzen*, Schriftenreihe des Bundesministeriums der Finanzen, Heft 64, Bonn.

Bond, S. R. and L. Chennells (2000), *Corporate Income Taxes and Investment: A Comparative Study*, The Institute for Fiscal Studies, London.

Caron & Stevens, Baker & McKenzie (1999), *Survey of the Effective Tax Burden in the European Union*, Amsterdam.

Chennells, L. and R. Griffith (1997), *Taxing Profits in a Changing World, The Institute for Fiscal Studies*, London.

Commission of the European Communities (1992), *Report of the Committee of Independent Experts on Company Taxation*, Brussels.

Deutsche Bank Research (1995), *Von der Pensionsrückstellung zum Pensionsfonds: Eine Chance für den deutschen Finanzmarkt*, Frankfurt.

Deutsche Bundesbank (1997a), Ertragslage und Finanzierungsverhältnisse ostdeutscher Unternehmen im Jahr 1995, *Monatsbericht* 7, 41-55.

Deutsche Bundesbank (1997b), Ertragslage und Finanzierungsverhältnisse westdeutscher Unternehmen im Jahr 1996, *Monatsbericht* 11, 31-55.

Deutsche Bundesbank (1997c), *Verhältniszahlen aus den Jahresabschlüssen westdeutscher Kapitalgesellschaften von 1987 bis 1995*, Frankfurt.

Devereux, M. (1992), The Impact of Taxation on International Business: Evidence from the Ruding Committee Survey, *EC Tax Review*, 105-117.

Devereux, M. and R. Griffith (1999), *The Taxation of Discrete Investment Choices (Revision 2)*, The Institute for Fiscal Studies, Working Paper Series No. W98/16, London.

Devereux, M. and L. Lammersen and Spengel C. (2000), *The Effective Levels of Company Taxation in the Member States of the EU*, Warwick, London, Mannheim.

Endres, D. and S. Ditsch (1999), German Corporate Tax Planning, *International Tax Journal*, Winter, 16-99.

Endres, D. and A. Oestreicher (2000), 2001 Tax Reform in Germany – Planning for a New Era, *Intertax*, 408-422.

European Council (2000), *Code of Conduct (Company Taxation)*, Primarolo Group, Brussels.

Gammie, M. (1997), The End of Imputation: Changes in UK Dividend Taxation, *Intertax*, 333-341.

Gammie, M. (1998), UK Imputation, Past, Present and Future, *IBFD Bulletin*, 429-439.

Hölscher, L. (1999), Das Problem der Einheitsbilanz. Handels- und Steuerbilanz in verschiedenen EU-Ländern, *Datenverarbeitung Steuern Wirtschaft Recht*, 302-307.

Industriekreditbank (1997), Hoffen auf Ertragswende – Mittelständische Unternehmen vor strategischer Neuorientierung, *IKB-Mitteilungen* 3, 18-23.

Jacobs, O. H. (1989), The Effects of Business Taxation on Shareholder Financing of Corporations – An Analysis of Taxation Concepts in France, Germany and the United States, *Intertax*, 464-476.

Jacobs, O. H. (1999), *Internationale Unternehmensbesteuerung*, München.

Jacobs, O. H. et al. (1999), *Eine vergleichende Untersuchung über die Besteuerung von Kapitalgesellschaften und ihrer Gesellschafter in Deutschland, Frankreich, Großbritannien, den Niederlanden und den Vereinigten Staaten*, Report on Behalf of the Ministry of Finance of Nordrhein-Westfalen, Mannheim.

Jacobs, O. H. and C. Spengel (1993), The Financing and Taxation of Corporations – A Comparing Analysis for the EC-Member Countries Germany, France and Great-Britain, *Intertax*, 1-15.

Jacobs, O. H. and C. Spengel (1996), *European Tax Analyzer*, Baden-Baden.

Jacobs, O. H. and C. Spengel (1997), Die Besteuerung in- und ausländischer Beteiligungserträge von Kapitalgesellschaften in Deutschland, Frankreich und Großbritannien, in: Kley, M.D. and Süner, E. and Willemsen, A. (Hrsg.), *Steuerrecht, Steuer- und Rechtspolitik, Wirtschaftsrecht und Unternehmensverfassung*, Umweltrecht, Festschrift für Wolfgang Ritter zum 70. Geburtstag, Köln, 115-145.

Jouanjan, A. (2000), France Plans FRF 120 Billion in Tax Cuts Over Three Years – What the Plan Entails, *Tax Notes International*, 1298-1299.

King. M. A. and D. Fullerton (1984), *The Taxation from Income of Capital*, Chicago.

Klein, H.-G. (1990), Bewertung von Versorgungsverpflichtungen nach englischem (SSAP 24), amerikanischem (FAS 87) und deutschem Recht, *Betriebliche Altersversorgung*, 130-136.

Kommission zur Reform der Unternehmensbesteuerung (1999), *Brühler Empfehlungen zur Reform der Unternehmensbesteuerung*, Schriftenreihe des Bundesministeriums der Finanzen, Heft 66, Bonn.

Küting, K. and M. Strickmann (1997), Die betriebliche Altersversorgung im Spannungsfeld von Bilanzpolitik und Bilanzanalyse, *Betriebs-Berater*, Beilage 12.

Kvist, J. (1992), *Taxation of Pensions in the EC*, Deventer.

Lefebvre, F. (2000), *Mémento Fiscal 2000*, Paris.

Luther, S. (1994), Steuern in der Investitionsrechnung und Unternehmensbewertung, *Jahrbuch Fachanwälte für Steuern*, 11-23.

Meyer, R. (1996), *Computergestützte Simulation von Steuerbelastungen*, Baden-Baden.

Monti, M. (1998), Die Integration des europäischen Finanzsektors: Die nächsten Schritte, *Wertpapiermanagement*, 1762-1765.

OECD (1985), *Two Reports by the Committee on Fiscal Affairs on Quantitative Aspects of Corporate Taxation*, Paris.

OECD (1991), *Taxing Profit in a Global Economy – Domestic and International Issues*, Paris.

OECD (1998), *Harmful Tax Competition, An Emerging Global Issue*, Paris.

OECD (2000a), *Tax Burdens: Alternative Measures*, Paris.

OECD (2000b), *Towards Global Tax Co-operation*, Report to the 2000 Ministerial Council Meeting and Recommendations by the Committee on Fiscal Affairs, Progress in Identifying and Eliminationg Harmful Tax Practices, Paris.

Oestreicher, A. and C. Spengel (1999), *Maßgeblichkeit der International Accounting Standards für die steuerliche Gewinnermittlung?*, Baden-Baden.

Rimbaux, E. (1996), Marginal Effective Tax Rates in Retrospect: 1970-1995, *Public Finance*, 92-127.

Ruhnke, K., M. Schmidt and T. Seidel (2000), Fortschritte bei der Verbreitung der IAS – Eine vorausschauende Zwischenbilanz, *Steuern und Bilanzen*, 876-883.

Seifert, M. (2000), Rechnungslegung in der EU – Umfassende Neuregelung?, *Steuern und Bilanzen*, 717-720.

Spengel, C. (1995), *Europäische Steuerbelastungsvergleiche*, Düsseldorf.

Statistisches Bundesamt (1997), *Statistisches Jahrbuch für die Bundesrepublik Deutschland 1997*, Wiesbaden.

Appendix A: Financial ratios of the different industries

Table A1: Financial Ratios of the different industries

	Return on turn-over %	Stocks to total balance sheet ratio %	Capital intensity %	Personnel intensity %	Equity ratio %	Return on equity %	Distribution ratio %
Manufacturing industry (Base case)	2.8	21.8	23.2	24.6	25.1	16.8	37.4
Chemical Engineering	3.5	8.6	20.1	25.0	40.9	10.0	51.9
Electrical Engineering	2.0	17.9	15.1	29.9	24.6	10.2	37.2
Food & Beverages	1.2	16.7	36.6	14.3	18.7	12.4	32.4
Automotive Vehicles	2.0	14.8	23.0	23.8	27.9	13.3	55.4
Engineering	2.1	6.3	15.9	31.6	20.9	13.3	39.8
Metal Production	2.0	24.6	29.1	22.8	24.8	12.4	11.3
Building & Construction	0.9	11.6	18.7	34.8	6.9	23.6	47.0
Service Trade	3.6	12.5	15.3	53.6	29.8	17.7	56.8
Commerce	1.0	35.4	15.7	10.6	10.5	23.6	46.0
Transport	2.1	0.9	54.1	29.3	17.4	15.3	38.7

Appendix B: Detailed results for the base case (section 2) and the sensitivity analysis (section 3) including the German Tax reform 2001 (section 4)

Table B1: Impact of types of taxes on the effective average tax rate - Only corporate taxes

EATR - corporation	FRA	GER	IRL	NL	UK	EU-5 Average
absolute in Euro	12,954,033	11,290,464	3,504,761	8,793,437	7,937,863	8,896,112
corporation tax and surcharges	7,037,881	8,689,994	2,704,136	8,659,264	7,033,418	6,824,939
trade/ franchise tax on income	-	2,517,630	-	-	-	503,526
trade tax on capital/ taxe professionnelle	4,199,789	-	-	-	-	839,958
employer´s contribution	1,385,938	-	-	-	-	277,188
property tax	-	-	-	-	-	-
real property tax	330,425	82,840	800,625	134,173	904,445	450,501
relative in %	100.0	100.0	100.0	100.0	100.0	100.0
corporation tax and surcharges	54.3	77.0	77.2	98.5	88.6	79.1
trade/ franchise tax on income	-	22.3	-	-	-	4.5
trade tax on capital/ taxe professionnelle	32.4	-	-	-	-	6.5
employer´s contribution	10.7	-	-	-	-	2.1
property tax	-	-	-	-	-	-
real property tax	2.6	0.7	22.8	1.5	11.4	7.8

Continuation Table B1:

EATR - corporation	USA	IRL 28%	GER 2001
absolute in Euro	10,480,517	7,706,237	10,503,163
corporation tax and surcharges	8,392,151	7,078,738	6,891,882
trade/ franchise tax on income	1,327,614	-	3,504,603
trade tax on capital/ taxe professionnelle	-	-	-
employer's contribution	-	-	-
property tax	760,752	-	-
real property tax	-	627,498	106,678
relative in %	100.0	100.0	100.0
corporation tax and surcharges	80.1	91.9	65.6
trade/ franchise tax on income	12.7	-	33.4
trade tax on capital/ taxe professionnelle	-	-	-
employer's contribution	-	-	-
property tax	7.2	-	-
real property tax	-	8.1	1.0

Table B2: Impact of types of taxes on the effective average tax rate - Corporate and personal taxes

EATR	FRA	GER	IRL	NL	UK	EU-5 Average
Corporation (Table A1)						
absolute in Euro	12,954,033	11,290,464	3,504,761	8,793,437	7,937,863	8,896,112
effective in %	39.7	32.8	8.3	24.0	21.0	25.2
Shareholder						
absolute in Euro	5,664,355	4,249,136	4,697,939	4,955,073	3,530,026	4,619,306
income tax	5,559,481	4,249,136	4,697,939	4,539,377	3,530,026	4,515,192
prroperty tax	104,874	--	--	415,696	--	104,114
Overall level						
absolute in Euro	18,618,388	15,539,600	8,202,700	13,748,510	11,467,888	13,515,417
effective in %	48.8	37.4	17.2	32.0	25.6	32.2

Continuation Table B2:

EATR	USA	IRL 28%	GER 2001/2005
Corporation (Table A1)			
absolute in Euro	10,480,517	7,706,237	10,503,163
effective in %	29.7	20.5	30.1
Shareholder			
absolute in Euro	3,306,954	4,697,939	2,674,425
income tax	3,256,842	4,697,939	2,674,425
property tax	50,112	--	--
Overall level			
absolute in Euro	13,787,471	12,404,176	13,177,588
effective in %	32.0	28.1	30.1

Table B3: Effective average tax rate across 5 EU Member States and the USA
- Variation of tangible fixed assets to total balance sheet ratio
- Only corporate taxes

Tangible fixed assets to total balance sheet-ratio %	18.3	19.5	20.6	21.8	22.9	24.0	25.2	26.3	27.5
FRA	30.7	31.2	31.9	32.8	33.6	33.9	34.8	36.0	36.6
GER	30.4	29.7	29.7	29.7	30.0	29.4	29.1	28.9	28.5
IRL	5.9	5.6	6.1	6.2	6.3	6.5	6.6	6.7	7.2
NED	17.8	17.7	17.9	17.8	17.8	17.3	17.6	17.6	17.4
UK	16.3	16.2	16.7	17.0	17.0	16.5	16.8	17.2	17.0
EU-5 Average	20.2	20.1	20.5	20.7	20.9	20.7	21.0	21.3	21.3
EU-5 Standard Deviation	9.4	9.5	9.4	9.6	9.8	9.8	9.9	10.2	10.2
GER 2001	21.9	21.4	21.7	22.0	22.1	21.8	21.7	21.8	21.7
IRL 28%	14.8	14.7	14.8	15.1	15.0	14.9	15.2	15.1	15.3
USA	21.9	21.8	21.7	22.0	22.1	21.8	22.1	22.2	22.1

Table B4: Effective average tax rate across 5 EU Member States and the USA
- Variation of equity to total capital ratio
- Only corporate taxes

Equity to total capital ratio %	25	50	75	100
FRA	43.1	43.9	44.2	44.7
GER	35.3	39.0	40.4	42.6
IRL	7.8	8.9	8.7	9.6
NED	21.0	23.6	26.0	27.7
UK	20.4	22.8	24.0	25.5
EU-5 Average	25.5	27.6	28.7	30.0
EU-5 Standard Deviation	12.4	12.5	12.7	12.8
GER 2001	27.5	29.3	30.8	31.9
IRL 28%	18.0	20.3	22.1	23.4
USA	26.3	29.3	30.8	33.0

Table B5: Effective average tax rate across 5 EU Member States and the USA
- Variation of pre tax return
- Only corporate taxes

Pre-tax return %	20.2	21.5	22.8	24.0	25.3	26.6	27.8	29.1	30.4
FRA	51.5	42.1	38.9	35.7	33.6	32.0	30.2	28.6	27.3
GER	31.2	30.8	30.5	30.3	30.0	29.7	29.1	28.6	28.3
IRL	7.9	7.5	7.1	6.6	6.3	6.0	5.8	5.5	5.6
NED	18.3	18.2	18.1	17.8	17.8	17.7	17.6	16.9	17.1
UK	18.3	17.8	17.7	17.0	17.0	16.5	16.2	15.9	15.5
EU-5 Average	25.4	23.3	22.5	21.5	20.9	20.4	19.8	19.1	18.8
EU-5 Standard Deviation	15.0	12.0	11.1	10.3	9.8	9.5	9.0	8.7	8.4
GER 2001	23.8	23.4	23.0	22.4	22.1	21.8	21.2	20.7	20.4
IRL 28%	16.8	16.4	15.9	15.4	15.0	15.0	14.7	14.1	14.1
USA	24.8	23.8	23.5	22.4	22.1	21.8	21.6	21.0	20.7

Table B6: Effective average tax rate across 5 EU Member States and the USA
- Different industries
- Differences with reference to the average EATR of the 5 EU Member States
- Only corporate taxes

Differences to EU-5	Transport	Commerce	Service Trade	Building and Construction	Metal Production	Engineering
FRA	36.4	37.0	40.5	102.2	83.7	64.0
GER	20.6	16.6	13.5	10.1	8.3	24.3
IRL	-26.2	-14.8	-21.5	-30.7	-56.8	-61.5
NED	5.2	-3.5	-10.8	-25.2	-21.2	-6.4
UK	-35.9	-35.3	-21.7	-36.2	-13.9	-20.4
EU-5 Standard Deviation	27.4	25.0	24.0	51.83	46.8	42.3
USA	27.6	12.1	8.4	-12.7	-1.2	11.4
GER 2001	33.3	11.4	12.3	-8.1	-3.6	16.7

Continuation Table B6:

Differences to EU-5	Automotive Vehicles	Food and Beverages	Electrical Engineering	Chemical Engineering	Manufacturing Industry
FRA	54.0	55.3	68.3	40.8	45.6
GER	23.5	12.9	24.2	27.3	26.9
IRL	-61.2	-53.5	-61.9	-58.7	-60.6
NED	-1.4	-9.3	-11.9	1.7	-1.2
UK	-15.0	-5.5	-18.7	-11.2	-10.7
EU-5 Standard Deviation	38.6	35.2	43.8	34.6	36.3
USA	17.6	8.6	9.9	30.5	17.8
GER 2001	29.8	9.1	17.4	28.7	18.0

Table B7: Effective average tax rate across 5 EU Member States and the USA
- Variation of rate of distribution
- Corporate and personal taxes

Distribution rate %	0	25	50	75	100
FRA	45.8	47.3	51.5	56.7	61.9
GER	37.4	37.4	40.1	42.8	46.7
IRL	12.3	18.2	24.8	32.3	41.1
NED	29.1	31.5	35.1	39.3	43.7
UK	22.7	25.6	28.7	32.3	36.0
EU-5 Average	29.5	32.0	36.0	40.7	45.9
EU-5 Standard Deviation	11.6	9.9	9.3	9.0	8.7
GER 2005	27.6	30.0	32.2	35.3	38.1
IRL 28%	22.2	27.6	34.2	41.3	49.2
USA	26.6	31.0	35.1	40.3	45.7

Table B8: Effective average tax rate across 5 EU Member States and the USA
- Variation of equity to total capital ratio
- Corporate and personal taxes

Equity to total capital ratio %	25	50	75	100
FRA	73.0	71.9	70.8	71.1
GER	55.1	55.1	56.2	56.5
IRL	49.4	49.4	48.3	48.9
NED	59.6	57.3	55.1	53.3
UK	42.7	42.7	43.8	44.4
EU-5 Average	56.0	55.3	54.8	54.8
EU-5 Standard Deviation	10.2	9.7	9.2	9.1
GER 2005	46.1	46.1	46.1	46.7
IRL 28%	53.9	55.1	56.2	58.9
USA	49.4	51.7	53.9	57.3

Appendix C: Changes of the effective average tax burden since 1995 (section 5)

Table C1: Effective average tax rate across 5 EU Member States and the USA
- Period 1995-2001
- Only corporate taxes

	1995	1996	1997	1998	1999	2000	2001
FRA	37.7	37.7	39.9	39.9	39.7	38.9	30.3
GER	38.2	38.2	38.2	36.8	32.8	32.8	30.1
IRL	6.6	6.6	7.4	7.4	8.3	8.3	8.3
NED	23.7	23.7	23.7	23.7	23.7	23.7	23.7
UK	21.5	21.5	21.5	19.7	21.0	21.0	21.0
EU-5 Average	25.5	25.5	26.1	25.5	25.1	24.9	22.7
EU-5 Standard Deviation	11.7	11.7	11.9	11.8	10.7	10.5	8.0
IRL 28%	21.8	21.8	21.0	22.3	20.5	17.5	17.5
USA	29.7	29.7	29.7	29.7	29.7	29.7	29.7

Table C2: Effective average tax rate across 5 EU Member States and the USA
- Period 1995-2001
- Corporate and personal taxes

	1995	1996	1997	1998	1999	2000	2001
FRA	45.3	45.3	46.5	48.7	48.8	47.8	40.2
GER	43.8	43.8	40.9	39.5	37.4	37.4	30.0
IRL	15.8	15.8	16.3	16.3	17.2	16.7	16.7
NED	38.3	38.3	32.6	31.9	32.0	32.0	32.0
UK	26.8	26.8	27.0	24.8	25.6	25.6	25.6
EU-5 Average	22.8	22.8	21.2	20.8	20.8	20.6	19.1
EU-5 Standard Deviation	12.8	12.8	10.6	10.1	9.0	9.2	7.2
IRL 28%	29.6	29.6	28.6	29.6	28.1	25.1	25.1
USA	32.0	32.0	32.0	32.0	32.0	32.0	32.0

Appendix D: Impact of hypothetical tax reforms in the EU (section 6)

Table D1: Results for simulations of reforming elements of the corporation tax base
- Effective average tax rates
- Only corporate taxes

	FRA	GER	IRL	NL	UK	EU-5 Average	EU-5 Stand. Dev.
Base case	39.7	30.1	8.3	24.0	21.0	24.6	10.4
1. Common depreciation on intangibles	39.7	30.1	8.3	24.0	21.0	24.6	10.4
2. Common depreciation on buildings	40.2	29.3	8.3	23.6	21.0	24.5	10.4
3. Common SL depreciation on tangible fixed assets	44.1	30.6	8.4	24.5	21.4	25.8	11.7
4. Common DB depreciation on tangible fixed assets	41.0	28.4	7.9	22.3	19.7	23.9	10.9
5. Common valuation of inventories	38.0	29.7	7.9	21.8	19.2	23.3	10.1
6. Common pension scheme (book reserve)	44.5	30.1	9.2	27.1	24.0	27.0	11.3
7. Common pension scheme (pension fund)	39.7	26.2	8.3	24.0	21.0	23.8	10.1
8. Common book reserves for bad debts	36.2	26.6	7.9	21.4	18.8	22.2	9.3
9. Common overall tax base (IAS)	46.7	29.7	8.7	24.5	21.4	26.2	12.4

Continuation Table D1:

	USA	GER 1999	IRL 28%
Base case	29.7	32.8	20.5
1. Common depreciation on intangibles	29.7	32.8	20.5
2. Common depreciation on buildings	28.8	32.8	20.5
3. Common SL depreciation on tangible fixed assets	32.3	36.7	20.6
4. Common DB depreciation on tangible fixed assets	29.8	32.8	19.2
5. Common valuation of inventories	27.5	32.8	18.8
6. Common pension scheme (book reserve)	34.1	32.8	22.7
7. Common pension scheme (pension fund)	29.7	27.5	20.5
8. Common book reserves for bad debts	26.6	28.8	18.3
9. Common overall tax base (IAS)	32.3	35.4	21.0

Table D2: Results for simulations of reforming elements of the corporation tax base
- Effective average tax rates
- Corporate and personal taxes

	FRA	GER	IRL	NL	UK	EU-5 Average	EU-5 Stand. Dev.
Base case	48.8	30.0	17.2	32.0	25.1	30.6	10.4
1. Common depreciation on intangibles	48.8	30.0	17.2	32.0	25.1	30.6	10.4
2. Common depreciation on buildings	49.3	30.0	17.2	31.5	25.6	30.7	10.5
3. Common SL depreciation on tangible fixed assets	52.7	31.0	17.2	32.5	25.6	31.8	11.7
4. Common DB depreciation on tangible fixed assets	49.8	29.1	16.7	30.5	24.1	30.0	11.0
5. Common valuation of inventories	46.8	30.0	16.7	30.0	24.1	29.5	9.9
6. Common pension scheme (book reserve)	53.2	30.0	17.2	35.0	27.6	32.6	11.8
7. Common pension scheme (pension fund)	48.8	27.1	17.7	32.0	25.6	30.2	10.4
8. Common book reserves for bad debts	45.3	27.6	16.7	29.6	23.6	28.6	9.5
9. Common overall tax base (IAS)	54.7	30.0	17.6	32.5	25.6	32.1	12.4

Continuation Table D2:

	USA	GER 1999	IRL 28%
Base case	32.0	37.4	28.1
1. Common depreciation on intangibles	32.0	37.4	28.1
2. Common depreciation on buildings	31.5	37.4	28.1
3. Common SL depreciation on tangible fixed assets	34.5	40.4	28.1
4. Common DB depreciation on tangible fixed assets	32.0	37.4	27.1
5. Common valuation of inventories	30.0	37.4	26.6
6. Common pension scheme (book reserve)	35.5	37.4	30.0
7. Common pension scheme (pension fund)	32.0	33.0	28.1
8. Common book reserves for bad debts	29.6	34.0	26.1
9. Common overall tax base (IAS)	34.0	39.9	28.6

Table D3: Results for simulations of reforming tax rates and local taxes
- Effective average tax rates
- Only corporate taxes

	FRA	GER	IRL	NL	UK	EU-5 Average	EU-5 Stand. Dev.
Base case	39.7	30.1	8.3	24.0	21.0	24.6	10.4
10. Common CT rate, at EU mean	36.7	34.1	23.6	21.8	22.7	27.8	6.3
11. Common CT rate incl. Local profit taxes, at EU mean	37.1	24.0	24.5	23.1	24.0	26.5	5.3
12. Common CT rate of 25% incl. local profit taxes	33.6	17.0	18.3	16.6	17.5	20.6	6.5
13. Common CT rate of 25% incl. all local taxes	9.6	17.0	16.2	16.2	14.8	14.8	2.7

Continuation Table D3:

	USA	GER 1999	IRL 28%
Base case	29.7	32.8	20.5
10. Common CT rate, at EU mean	28.4	25.8	-
11. Common CT rate incl. Local profit taxes, at EU mean	25.3	17.0	-
12. Common CT rate of 25% incl. local profit taxes	19.7	12.2	-
13. Common CT rate of 25% incl. all local taxes	16.2	12.2	-

Table D4: Results for simulations of reforming tax rates and local taxes
- Effective average tax rates
- Corporate and personal taxes

	FRA	GER	IRL	NL	UK	EU-5 Average	EU-5 Stand. Dev.
Base case	48.8	30.0	17.2	32.0	25.1	30.6	10.4
10. Common CT rate, at EU mean	45.8	33.0	31.0	30.0	27.1	33.4	6.5
11. Common CT rate incl. local profit taxes, at EU mean	46.3	25.1	32.0	31.0	27.6	32.4	7.4
12. Common CT rate of 25% incl. local profit taxes	43.3	20.2	26.1	25.6	22.7	27.6	8.1
13. Common CT rate of 25% incl. all local taxes	21.7	20.2	24.6	25.1	20.2	22.4	2.1

Continuation Table D4:

	USA	GER 1999	IRL 28%
Base case	32.0	37.4	28.1
10. Common CT rate, at EU mean	31.0	31.0	-
11. Common CT rate incl. local profit taxes, at EU mean	28.6	23.6	-
12. Common CT rate of 25% incl. local profit taxes	23.6	19.7	-
13. Common CT rate of 25% incl. all local taxes	20.7	19.2	-

Table D5: Results for corporation tax system reform simulations
- Effective average tax rates
- Corporate and personal taxes

	FRA	GER	IRL	NL	UK	EU-5 Average	EU-5 Stand. Dev.
Base case (only corporate taxes)	39.7	30.1	8.3	24.0	21.0	24.6	10.4
Base case (corporate and personal taxes)	48.8	31.0	17.2	32.0	25.6	30.9	10.4
14. Common CT system, classical system (only corporate taxes)	48.0	30.1	8.3	24.0	21.0	26.3	13.0
15. Common CT system, classical system (corporate and personal taxes)	55.7	32.0	17.2	37.4	26.6	33.8	12.8

Continuation Table D5:

	USA	GER 1999	IRL 28%
Base case (only corporate taxes)	29.7	32.8	20.5
Base case (corporate and personal taxes)	32.0	37.4	28.1
14. Common CT system, classical system (only corporate taxes)	29.7	38.4	20.5
15. Common CT system, classical system (corporate and personal taxes)	32.0	40.9	28.1

List of Figures

List of Tables

GPSR Compliance

The European Union's (EU) General Product Safety Regulation (GPSR) is a set of rules that requires consumer products to be safe and our obligations to ensure this.

If you have any concerns about our products, you can contact us on ProductSafety@springernature.com

In case Publisher is established outside the EU, the EU authorized representative is:

Springer Nature Customer Service Center GmbH
Europaplatz 3
69115 Heidelberg, Germany

Batch number: 10725973

Printed by Printforce, the Netherlands